PRODUCERS CIRCLE

LAVENDER, HYACINTH, VIOLET, YEW
by Coral Wylie

Lavender, Hyacinth, Violet, Yew premiered at the Bush Theatre, London, on 8 February 2025.

LAVENDER, HYACINTH, VIOLET, YEW
by Coral Wylie

Cast
Pip	Coral Wylie
Lorin	Pooky Quesnel
Craig	Wil Johnson
Duncan	Omari Douglas

Creative Team

Director	Debbie Hannan
Set & Costume Designer	Max Johns
Lighting Designer	Laura Howard
Sound Designer & Composer	Holly Khan
Movement Director	Annie-Lunnette Deakin-Foster
Design Associate and Costume Supervisor	Maariyah Sharjil
Bush Associate Dramaturg	Titilola Dawudu
Casting Director	Jatinder Chera
Voice Coach	Joel Trill
Production Dramatherapy	Wabriya King
Botanical Designer	Dan Yeo
Production Manager	Jack Boissieux for JBPM
Company Stage Manager	Rebecca Natalini
Assistant Stage Manager	Jasmine Dittman
RADA Stage Management Placement	Danielle Adams
Production Carpenter	Jay Williamson
Production Electrician	Adam Wileman
Production Sound Engineer	Sasha Howe
Production Assistant	Ida Pontoppidan for JBPM
Lighting Programmer	Jennifer Garland
Scenic Artist	Lauren Cahill
Scenic Artist	Susanna Burton
Set Construction	Centreline Fabrications
Lighting Rental	White Light

With special thanks to Clyde Cooper, Jerwood Foundation, The Royal Victoria Hall Foundation, EJS Couriers, White Light and Diane Wilmott-Stiles.

Cast

Coral Wylie | Pip

Coral Wylie is the writer of *Lavender, Hyacinth, Violet, Yew*, and plays Pip.

Coral (they/them) is a writer, performer and theatre maker from West London. Their work finds its voice in the natural world (most often bugs...), playing in the overlaps of science and art. A founding member of the Bush Theatre's Young Company, Coral's work has been performed on the theatre's main stage within their 2022 show *ANTHEM*. As a part of Soho Theatre Writers' Lab, they wrote their first full length script, *ENTOMOLOGY*, which was longlisted for the Tony Craze Award 2022. Most recently, Coral was invited to join the Bush Theatre's Emerging Writers' Group, where they developed their current script *Lavender, Hyacinth, Violet, Yew*, which was then shortlisted for The Alfred Fagon Award 2023 before being programmed as part of the theatre's 2024/25 season.

Pooky Quesnel | Lorin

Pooky is widely recognised for her role as Louise in three seasons of BBC's *The A Word* and its spin-off series *Ralph and Katie*. She recently portrayed Pauline Treherne/Maureen Gardner in BBC series *Moonflower Murders*, Louise Fitzallan in *Beyond Paradise*, and Enid in ITV's *The Larkins*. Additional credits include Mrs Linux in *The Confessions of Frannie Langton*, Mo Buckley in *The Victim*, Olga in *Waterloo Road*, Mandy in Sky's *Two Weeks to Live*, and Maz in the BBC series *Ladhood*.

On stage, Pooky starred as Tracey in *Sweat* (Royal Exchange, Manchester); *Min in The Suicide* (National Theatre) and Martha in *Who's Afraid of Virginia Woolf* (Tobacco Factory, Bristol). She has also performed at esteemed venues such as the Sam Wanamaker Playhouse, Almeida Theatre and Bristol Old Vic. Beyond acting, Pooky's screenwriting portfolio includes credits on *Casualty*, *Doctors*, and projects in collaboration with the National Theatre Studio.

Wil Johnson | Craig

Theatre credits include: *The Merry Wives of Windsor*, *The School for Scandal* (RSC); *Shed: Exploded View* (Royal Exchange, Manchester); *Jitney, Rosencrantz & Guildenstern are Dead* (Old Vic); *Running with Lions* (Lyric Hammersmith); *Women Beware Women* (Sam Wannamaker Playhouse); *Glengarry Glen Ross* (UK Tour); *Sweat*

(Donmar Warehouse/Giegud Theatre); *Leave Taking* (Bush Theatre); *King Lear* (Royal Exchange, Manchester); *A Wolf in Snakeskin Shoes* (Tricycle Theatre); *The Great Goat Bubble* (Druid Theatre, Ireland); *The Queen & I* (Vaudeville Theatre); *Shallowing Dark* (Theatre503); *Serious Money* (Birmingham Rep); *Torn* (Arcola); *Wild Turkey* (Troxy Bar); *Redundant* (Royal Court); *Othello* (Royal Lyceum, Edinburgh); *Twelfth Night* (International Tour); *Running Dream* (Theatre Royal Stratford East); *Fuente Ovejuna* (National Theatre); *The Bacchae* (Shared Experience).

Television credits include: *Cobra: Rebellion*, *The Five* (Sky); *House of the Dragon* (HBO Max); *The Larkins* (Of Productions/ITV); *Death in Paradise* (Red Planet/BBC); *Carnival Row* (Legendary Television); *Outlander* (Lionsgate/Amazon); *Moving On* (BBC); *Lewis*, *Emmerdale*, *Vera*, *Buried Treasure*, *Cracker*, *Anna Lee*, *The Bill*, *London's Burning* (ITV); *Hetty Feather*, *Holby City*, *Waterloo Road*, *Waking the Dead*, *Clocking Off*, *Babyfather*, *Starting Out* (BBC).

Film credits include: *Tell No Lies* (Tubi Originals); *Macbeth* (Green Screen Productions); *In a Better World* (Zentropa); *Dead End* (Ocean Storm Films); *Anuvahood* (Revolver); *Pimp* (Triple S Films); *Adulthood* (Adulthood Limited); *Yes* (Adventure Pictures); *South West 9* (Fruit Salad Films); *Babymother* (Film Four); *Emotional Backgammon* (Epicum Films).

Omari Douglas | Duncan

Omari is a BAFTA and Olivier-nominated actor. He most recently starred in Joe Barton's series for Netflix, *Black Doves*, alongside Keira Knightley and Ben Whishaw. He is well known for his breakthrough role in Russell T Davies' smash hit series, *It's A Sin* (Channel 4/HBO Max) for which he received a BAFTA nomination for Best Supporting Actor. His other screen highlights include *I Hate Suzie Too* (Sky), *Nolly* (ITV) and the Searchlight feature film, *Rye Lane*.

On stage, he was recently seen in Ivo Van Hove's *A Little Life* (Harold Pinter Theatre, Savoy Theatre). He also starred in *Cabaret* at the Kit Kat Club, opposite Jessie Buckley and Eddie Redmayne. His role in *Constellations* (Vaudeville Theatre) opposite Russell Tovey led to an Olivier Award nomination for Best Actor. Other theatre credits include: *White Rabbit, Red Rabbit* (sohoplace); *Romantics Anonymous* (Bristol Old Vic); *Wise Children*, *High Society* (Old Vic); *Rush* (King's Head); *Peter Pan*, *Jesus Christ Superstar* (Regent's Park Open Air); *Five Guys Named Moe* (Marble Arch); *Tristan & Yseult* (Kneehigh/Shakespeare's Globe); *The Life* (Southwark Playhouse); *Annie Get Your Gun* (Sheffield Crucible); *Hairspray* (Curve).

CREATIVE TEAM

Coral Wylie | Writer

Coral (they/them) is a writer, performer and theatre maker from West London. Their work finds its voice in the natural world (most often bugs...), playing in the overlaps of science and art. A founding member of the Bush Theatre's Young Company, Coral's work has been performed on the theatre's main stage within their 2022 show *ANTHEM*. As a part of Soho Theatre Writers' Lab, they wrote their first full length script, *ENTOMOLOGY*, which was longlisted for the Tony Craze Award 2022. Most recently, Coral was invited to join the Bush Theatre's Emerging Writers' Group, where they developed their current script *Lavender, Hyacinth, Violet, Yew*, which was then shortlisted for The Alfred Fagon Award 2023 before being programmed as part of the theatre's 2024/25 season.

Debbie Hannan | Director

Debbie Hannan writes and directs for stage and screen. They are currently Associate Director at National Theatre of Scotland, and Associate Artist at Cardboard Citizens. They were formerly Interim Artistic Director at Stockroom, theatre's first writers room. They trained at the Royal Conservatoire of Scotland and as Trainee Director at the Royal Court, and recently joined the board of Theatre Uncut.

They have directed at theatres such as the Royal Court Theatre, the Young Vic, the Bush Theatre, Soho Theatre, the Royal Exchange (Manchester), the Tron Theatre (Glasgow), the Citizens Theatre (Glasgow), the Traverse Theatre (Edinburgh), and have worked with companies such as Complicité, Clean Break, Sonia Friedman Productions and Paines Plough, and won an Olivier as Associate Director for Best Revival of Constellations on the West End.

Theatre credits include: *Sound of the Underground* (Royal Court), *The Panopticon* (National Theatre of Scotland) and *Overflow* (Bush Theatre). They received the Genesis New Director's Award, and an MGCfutures Bursary. As a writer, they have been commissioned by Cardboard Citizens for the More Than One Story project, were recently shortlisted for the Alpine Fellowship Playwriting Award, are writing a new musical developed by Northern Stage, and are adapting a children's book for the Unicorn Theatre.

Debbie has directed a short produced by Film4 and 104 Films, co-written with Matilda Ibini, which screened at London Film Festival 2023. They were Shadow Director on Shetland Season six and seven, and are developing a feature on a BFI Creative Challenge Lab. Debbie is now writing their first feature, with research supported by the Miles Ketley Memorial Fund.

Max Johns | Set & Costume Designer

Max Johns trained in theatre design at Bristol Old Vic Theatre School and was the recipient of a BBC Performing Arts Fellowship in 2015, and prior to this he worked for a number of years as a designer in Germany.

Theatre credits include: costume design for *Why Am I So Single?* (Garrick); *The Duchess [Of Malfi]* co-design with Tom Piper (The Trafalgar); *As You Like It* (Shakespeare's Globe); *Sound Of The Underground* co-design with Rosie Elnile (Royal Court Theatre); *Choir Boy*, *Birthmarked*, *Life Raft*, *Medusa*, *The Light Burns Blue*, *Under A Cardboard Sea* (Bristol Old Vic); *The Climbers* (Theatre by the Lake); *The P Word*, *Overflow*, *Strange Fruit* and *Rust* (Bush Theatre); *The Strange Undoing Of Prudencia Hart* (Royal Exchange, Manchester); *Once Upon A Time In Nazi Occupied Tunisia* (Almeida); *King John* (RSC); *The Panopticon* (National Scotland); *Lord Of The Flies*, *Kes* and *Random* (Leeds Playhouse); *Heartbreakin'* (WLB Esslingen, Germany); *Buggy Baby* (Yard); *Yellowman* (Young Vic); *The Half God Of Rainfall* (Kiln/Birmingham Rep/Fuel); *Urinetown* (Central School of Speech and Drama); *Wendy and Peter Pan* (The Royal Lyceum Edinburgh); *Utility*, *Twelfth Night* (Orange Tree); *Fidelio* (London Philharmonic Orchestra); *Enron*, *Our Town* (the Egg); *Hamlet* and *All's Well That Ends Well* (Shakespeare at the Tobacco Factory).

Laura Howard | Lighting Designer

Laura (she/they) graduated from the University of Exeter with a BSc in Biological Sciences before gaining a Distinction in Production and Technical Arts at LAMDA as a recipient of the William and Katherine Longman Charitable Trust Scholarship. Often working in new writing, Laura's work is led by story, whilst also offering bold, atmospheric, and artistic designs.

Theatre credits include: *Elephant, This Might Not Be It, Invisible, Clutch* and *The Kola Nut Does Not Speak English* (Bush Theatre); *The Legend of Ned Ludd* (Liverpool Everyman); *Bangers* (Arcola Theatre); *Odyssey: A Heroic Pantomime* (Jermyn Street Theatre); *Salty Irina* (Paines Plough Roundabout); *Dismissed* and *Splintered* (Soho Theatre); *Manorism* (Southbank Centre), *The Beach House* (Park Theatre); *Exodus* (National Theatre of Scotland).

Holly Khan | Sound Designer & Composer

Holly is a British/Guyanese composer, sound designer and multi-instrumentalist, creating scores for theatre, film and installation.

Theatre credits include: *Statues*, *Dreaming and Drowning* (Bush Theatre); *Our Country's Good* (Lyric Hammersmith); *Sam Wu is not*

Afraid of Ghosts (Polka Children's); *Sylvia* (English Theatre Frankfurt GMBH); *Bellringers* – OFFIE-nominated for Best Sound Design), the Olivier-nominated *Blackout Songs, This Much I Know, Biscuits for Breakfast* (Hampstead Theatre); *Tess* (Turtle Key Arts/Sadler's Wells); *I Really Do Think This Will Change Your Life* (Colchester Mercury); *Duck* (Arcola Theatre); *Northanger Abbey, Red Speedo* (Orange Tree Theatre); *The Invincibles* (Queen's Hornchurch); *Unseen Unheard* (Theatre Peckham); *Laughing Boy, Jules and Jim* (Jermyn Street Theatre); *Mansfield Park* (The Watermill); *The Beach House* (Park Theatre); *For A Palestinian* (Bristol Old Vic/Camden People's – OFFIE nominated for Best Sound Design); *Amal Meets Alice* (Good Chance Company, The Story Museum); *Kaleidoscope* (Filskit Company, Southbank Centre/Oxford Playhouse); *Ticker* (Alphabetti, Newcastle/Underbelly, Edinburgh/Theatre503).

Film and installation credits include: *Becoming An Artist: Bhajan Hunjan* (Tate Kids); *One Day* (Blind Summit, Anne Frank Trust); *Sanctuary* (Limbic Cinema, Stockton Arts Festival); *Song for the Metro* (The Sage Music Centre, Newcastle); *It's About Time* (UN Women/Battersea Arts Centre/Mayor of London); *Their Voices* (RAA & Global Health Film Festival, Barbican).

Annie-Lunnette Deakin-Foster | Movement Director

Annie-Lunnette Deakin-Foster is a London-based Movement Director and Choreographer.

Theatre credits include: *Romeo & Juliet* (Belgrade Theatre/Bristol Old Vic/Hackney Empire); *Treasure Island* (Orange Tree); *Pericles* (RSC/Chicago); *Richard, my Richard* (Shakespeare North); *A Midsummer Night's Dream* (RSC/Barbican); *Othello* (Shakespeare's Globe); *Sleeping Beauty* (Theatr Clywd); *The Little Matchgirl and Happier Tales* (Wise Children); *Beautiful Thing* (Stratford East/Leeds Playhouse/HOME Manchester); *The Tempest Reimagined* (Regent's Park Open Air/Unicorn); *A Midsummer Night's Dream* (Shakespeare's Globe); *The Flood* (Queen's); *You Bury Me* (Bristol Old Vic/UK tour); *Lemons Lemons, Lemons, Lemons, Lemons* (Harold Pinter); *The Famous Five* (Chichester Festival/Theatr Clwyd); *Heart* (Minetta Lane, New York); *Romeo & Juliet/Little Women* (Grosvenor Park Open Air); *An Octoroon* (Abbey); *Cock* (Ambassadors); *Mum* (Soho/ Royal Plymouth); *Rockets and Blue Lights* (National); *Robin Hood, Beauty And The Beast, The Panto That Nearly Never Was, Pavilion* (Theatr Clwyd); *Black Victorians* (National Tour); *Overflow, Chiaroscuro* (Bush); *The Bee in Me, Aesop's Fables, Grimm Tales* (Unicorn); *You Stupid Darkness!* (Southwark Playhouse); *The Last Noel* (Arts at the Old Fire Station/UK tour); *On The Other Hand We're Happy, Daughterhood, Dexter* and *Winters Detective Agency* (Paines Plough Roundabout); *Pop Music* (National Tour); *The Court Must Have a Queen* (Hampton Court Palace); *The Little Prince* (Omnibus).

Maariyah Sharjil | Design Associate and Costume Supervisor

Maariyah Sharjil is a designer and a recent first-class graduate from BA Design for Performance at the Royal Central School of Speech and Drama (2021). Before her design training, Maariyah worked at Sands Films as a costume constructor.

Theatre credits include: Costume researcher for *Life of Pi* (American Repertory); Design associate and costume supervisor for *The P-Word* (Bush Theatre); Assistant Costume Supervisor for *The Father and the Assassin* (National Theatre); Costume Designer for *The Key Workers' Cycle* (Almeida Theatre).

Jatinder Chera | Casting Director

For Bush Theatre: Olivier Award-winning *Sleepova* and *The P Word*, *The Real Ones*, and Olivier Award-nominated *A Playlist for The Revolution*.

Theatre credits include: *G* (Royal Court); *The Comeuppance* (Almeida Theatre); *The Flea, Samuel Takes a Break...*, *Multiple Casualty Incident* (Yard Theatre); *Sweat* (Royal Exchange, Manchester).

Dan Yeo | Botanical Designer

Dan Yeo, founder of Plants by Dan, specialises in creating stunning botanical designs for urban spaces. His expertise has been sought after by a wide array of clients in major retail, fashion and hospitality spaces in London and Bristol. Drawing inspiration from the natural world, Dan's installations cultivate lush and unique oases within urban settings.

Jack Boissieux for JBPM | Production Manager

Jack runs a production management company working across theatre, opera, dance, musicals and events. He has worked on national and international touring productions, West End musicals and immersive / site specific theatre.

Theatre credits include: *The Choir of Man* (West End/International tour); *Bluey's Big Play* (International tour); Head of Production at Waterperry Opera Festival; *Pied Piper* (National tour); *Feeling Afraid As If Something Terrible Is Going To Happen* (Bush Theatre/International tour); *A Very Naughty Christmas* (Southwark Playhouse/Elephant); *Wilko* (Queen's Hornchurch); *Lay Down Your Burdens* (Barbican/National tour); *The Ancient Oak of Baldor* (National tour); *Lost Lending Library and A Curious*

Quest (Punchdrunk); *Maddie Moate's Very Curious Christmas* (West End); *Berlusconi* (Southwark Playhouse/Elephant); *The Borrowers* (Theatre By The Lake); *An Improbable Musical* (National tour); *Habibti Driver* (Octagon Theatre); *Saving Face* (Curve/ National tour); *LAVA* (Soho Theatre/National tour) and the Annual Fundraising Gala for the National Youth Theatre.

Rebecca Natalini | Company Stage Manager

Rebecca Natalini graduated with a BA in Stage Management from the Royal Central School of Speech and Drama and she is working at the Bush Theatre for the second time after working on *The Real Ones*.

Theatre credits include: *The Real Ones* (Bush Theatre); *Pride and Prejudice, Scenes from RENT – A Staged Performance* (Curve); *A Midsummer Night's Dream* (New Diorama); *Zoe's Peculiar Journey Through Time* (UK and Norway tour); *Pride & Prejudice* (*sort of)* (UK tour).

Jasmine Dittman | Assistant Stage Manager

Lavender, Hyacinth, Violet, Yew is Jasmine's first show at the Bush. After several years working on arts festivals, she trained in stage and production management in Edinburgh and works across theatre and festivals.

Theatre credits include: *The Years* (Almeida) and *Boys on the Verge of Tears* (Soho).

Jennifer Garland | Lighting Programmer

Jen Garland graduated from LAMDA in 2024 with a degree in Production and Technical Arts, specialising in Lighting.

Theatre credits: *Stranger Things: The First Shadow* (West End); *Machinal, Wolfie, Suite in Three Keys* (Orange Tree); *The Great Christmas Feast, 58th Street Country Club* (The Lost Estate); *Royal Variety Performance, Festival of Rememberance* (Royal Albert Hall). As well as various performances at Opera Holland Park and the Royal Court.

TV and film credits: *Behind the Mountain* (Advert, Paramount Pictures); *Graham Norton, Strictly Come Dancing, The Joy Awards, EA FC Pro* (Light Initiative).

Bush Theatre

We make theatre for London. Now.

For over 50 years the Bush Theatre has been a world-famous home for new plays and an internationally renowned champion of playwrights.

Combining ambitious artistic programming with meaningful community engagement work and industry leading talent development schemes, the Bush Theatre champions and supports unheard voices to develop the artists and audiences of the future.

Since opening in 1972 the Bush has produced more than 500 ground-breaking premieres of new plays, developing an enviable reputation for its acclaimed productions nationally and internationally.

They have nurtured the careers of writers including James Graham, Lucy Kirkwood, Temi Wilkey, Jonathan Harvey and Jack Thorne. Recent successes include Tyrell Williams' *Red Pitch*, Benedict Lombe's *Shifters*, and Arinzé Kene's *Misty*. The Bush has won over 100 awards including the Olivier Award for Outstanding Achievement in Affliate Theatre for the past four years for Richard Gadd's *Baby Reindeer*, Igor Memic's *Old Bridge*, Waleed Akhtar's *The P Word* and Matilda Feyiṣayọ Ibini's *Sleepova*.

Located in the renovated old library on Uxbridge Road in the heart of Shepherd's Bush, the Bush Theatre continues to create a space where all communities can be part of its future and call the theatre home.

> **'The place to go for ground-breaking work as diverse as its audiences'** EVENING STANDARD

bushtheatre.co.uk
@bushtheatre

h&f hammersmith & fulham

Supported by ARTS COUNCIL ENGLAND

Artistic Director	Lynette Linton
Executive Director	Mimi Findlay
Associate Artistic Director	Daniel Bailey
Deputy Executive Director	Angela Wachner
Development & Marketing Assistant	Nicima Abdi
Head of Marketing	Shannon Clarke
Head of Development	Jocelyn Cox
Associate Dramaturg	Titilola Dawudu
Finance Assistant	Lauren Francis
Resident Director & Young Company Director	Katie Greenall
Technical & Buildings Manager	Jamie Haigh
Freelance Producer	Emma Halstead
Assistant Venue Manager	Rae Harm
Head of Finance	Neil Harris
Marketing Officer	Laela Henley-Rowe
Lead Producer	Nikita Karia
Community Producing Assistant	Joanne Leung
Event Sales Manager	Simon Pilling
Senior Technician	John Pullig
Production Technician	Charlie Sadler
Venue Manager (Theatre)	Ade Seriki
Press Manager	Martin Shippen
Community Producer	Holly Smith
Literary & Producing Assistant	Laetitia Somè
Marketing Manager	Ed Theakston
Marketing Officer	Kelly Thurston
Assistant Venue Manager (Box Office)	Robin Wilks
Theatre Administrator & Executive Assistant	Chloe Wilson
Café Bar Manager	Wayne Wilson

DUTY MANAGERS
Sara Dawood, Molly Elson, Thomas Ingram, Madeleine Simpson-Kent & Anna-May Wood.

VENUE SUPERVISORS
Antony Baker, Addy Caulder-James, Stephanie Cremona, Emma Chatel, Zea Hilland, Nzuzi Malemda, Roy Mas, Jacob Meier & Louis Nicholson.

VENUE ASSISTANTS
Javine Aduganfi, Doridan Bavangila, Charlotte Binns, Will Byam-Shaw, Pyerre Clarke, Daniel Fesoom, Matias Hailu, Bo Leandro, Maya Li Preti, Ishani McGuire, Khy Matinez, April Miller, Ed Mendoza, Carys Murray, Chana Nardone, Jennifer Okolo, James Robertson, Ali Shah & Nefertari Williams.

BOARD OF TRUSTEES
Uzma Hasan (Chair), Mark Dakin, Kim Evans, Keerthi Kollimada, Lynette Linton, Anthony Marraccino, Jim Marshall, Rajiv Nathwani, Kwame Owusu, Stephen Pidcock & Catherine Score.

Bush Theatre, 7 Uxbridge Road, London W12 8LJ
Box Office: 020 8743 5050 | Administration: 020 8743 3584
Email: info@bushtheatre.co.uk | bushtheatre.co.uk

Alternative Theatre Company Ltd
The Bush Theatre is a Registered Charity and a company limited by guarantee.
Registered in England no. 1221968 Charity no. 270080

THANK YOU

Our supporters make our work possible. Together, we're evolving the canon and creating a bolder, more diverse, and representative future for British theatre. We're so grateful to you all.

MAJOR DONORS
Charles Holloway OBE
Jim & Michelle Gibson
Georgia Oetker
Cathy & Tim Score
Susie Simkins
Jack Thorne
Gianni & Michael Alen-Buckley

SHOOTING STARS
Jim & Michelle Gibson
Anthony Marraccino & Mariela Manso
Cathy & Tim Score
Susie Simkins

LONE STARS
Clyde Cooper
Adam Kenwright
Jim Marshall
Georgia Oetker

HANDFUL OF STARS
Charlie Bigham
Judy Bollinger
Christopher delaMare
David des Jardins
Sue Fletcher
Thea Guest
Kate Hamer Ltd
Elizabeth Jack
Simon & Katherine Johnson
Joanna Kennedy
Garry & Lorna Lawrence
Phyllida Lloyd & Kate Pakenham
Vivienne Lukey
Sam & Jim Murgatroyd
Mark & Anne Paterson

Nick & Annie Reid
Bhagat Sharma
Dame Emma Thompson
Joe Tinston & Amelia Knott

RISING STARS
Elizabeth Beebe
Matthew Cushen
Anne-Hélène and Rafaël Biosse Duplan
Martin Blackburn
David Brooks
Catharine Browne
Anthony Chantry
Lauren Clancy
Richard & Sarah Clarke
Caroline Clasen
Susan Cuff
Austin Erwin
Kim Evans
Mimi Findlay
Jack Gordon
Hugh & Sarah Grootenhuis
Sarah Harrison
Uzma Hasan
Lesley Hill & Russ Shaw
Davina & Malcolm Judelson
Mike Lewis
Lynette Linton
Tim & Deborah Maunder
Michael McCoy
Judy Mellor
Caro Millington
Rajiv Nathwani
Yoana Nenova
Stephen Pidcock
Miguel & Valeri Ramos Handal
James St. Ville KC

Jan Topham
Kit & Anthony van Tulleken
Evanna White
Ben Yeoh

CORPORATE SPONSORS
Biznography
Casting Pictures Ltd.
Nick Hern Books
S&P Global
The Agency

TRUSTS & FOUNDATIONS
Backstage Trust
Buffini Chao Foundation
Christina Smith Foundation
Daisy Trust
Esmée Fairbairn Foundation
The Foyle Foundation
Garfield Weston Foundation
Garrick Charitable Trust
Hammersmith United Charities
The Harold Hyam Wingate Foundation
Idlewild Trust
Jerwood Foundation
John Lyon's Charity
Martin Bowley Charitable Trust
Noël Coward Foundation
Royal Victoria Hall Foundation
The Thistle Trust

And all the donors who wish to remain anonymous.

If you are interested in finding out how to be involved, please visit **bushtheatre.co.uk/support-us** email **development@bushtheatre.co.uk** or call **020 8743 3584**.

LAVENDER, HYACINTH, VIOLET, YEW

Coral Wylie

For Camilla, always for Camilla.

And for Wayne,

Thanks for the jacket.
We would've given them hell.

'Few understand the importance of having a sick ass jacket that everyone recognizes you by'

Twitter User @chaiconsumer, 2022

Characters

LORIN (*she/her*), *Pip's mum. Fifties, white, cis woman*
CRAIG (*he/him*), *Pip's dad. Fifties, Black Caribbean, raised in London, cis man*
PIP (*they/them*), *their child. Early twenties, Black/mixed race, non-binary*
DUNCAN (*he/him*), *the missing piece. Barely thirties, Black Caribbean, raised in Brum, cis man*

Casting does *not* need to be realistic but should feel playful, imaginative and reflect the diversity of identities that are oppressed by patriarchy.

Notes on the Text

An asterisk (*) indicates the start and two (**) indicate the end of a diary entry. These can be performed live or recorded. They may be spoken by one, or multiple, characters or voices. Lines of ~~strikethrough text~~ are indicative of a change of mind and/or re-drafting of the diary entry. <u>Underlined text</u> indicates text that has been physically underlined by the diary writer. These elements should be expressed however the performers see fit. Queer their method of delivery!

Overlapping dialogue is indicated with a forward slash (/).

This text went to press before the end of rehearsals and so may differ slightly from the play as performed.

ACT ONE

*

'Dear Diary,

Weird one today. Found the most amazing bamboo chair on Freecycle, going to ask Dad if I can put it in the garden. No prizes for guessing how that will go.

Three months on from the great uni drop-out and life at home is still… sticky.

She texted me, actually.

Said we 'left too much unsaid'.

I blocked her number. Then unblocked it. Then blocked it again. We stand firm.

My focus is on tonight. Bought birthday card. Bevvies from Tesco. Nearly got my septum pierced but I'm trying to practise patience and good decision-making – we'll see how long that lasts.

Mostly it was because I caught sight of the guy at the piercing place. Thick, long eyelashes fluttering over a sharp, hard jaw.

I'm right back here again.

I want to be feminine the way a man gets to be feminine. I want to put on a corset and jeans and look like a fucking rockstar – not like a sixteen-year-old who just watched Gentleman Jack *for the first time.*

Why can't I experiment with being femme?

Why is it my norm?

Why can't I express myself through femininity instead of it just being my default?

If I want to be masc, I take stuff off. I strip myself back.

How do I express myself by just taking things away?

I don't like myself. I don't know myself. I don't know how to fix it.

Also, this isn't a cry for help but I'm thinking about shaving my head.

– Pip'

**

Lorin and Craig

The kitchen. A pile of plantain on the table. LORIN *is in her pyjamas and slippers, fighting with a set of very old stepladders, and it appears the ladders are winning.* CRAIG *storms through, fully dressed down to muddy boots. He pulls a pair of gardening gloves out of a drawer and turns back around to exit – the drawer notably left wide open.*

LORIN. Are you out this morning?

CRAIG. Allotment.

LORIN. Oh.

CRAIG. What?

LORIN. I need help with the loft.

CRAIG. You don't need me for that.

LORIN. It's too high, and these ladders are older than me, I'm pretty sure.

CRAIG. Artefacts that old belong in a museum.

    LORIN *swings the ladders back threateningly at* CRAIG, *he giggles and runs to the other side of the room.*

LORIN. You said you'd help.

ACT ONE 9

CRAIG. It's minus-two, Lori, I have to cover the ground before it frosts.

LORIN. Most people would hear it's minus-two and take that as a clear sign to stay at home.

CRAIG (*not listening*). Mm.

LORIN. When will you be back?

CRAIG. I'm not sure – you and Pippa pick a takeaway though.

LORIN. Okay... It's Pip, remember?

CRAIG. What?

LORIN. Pip. No 'a'.

CRAIG. Right.

LORIN. Seriously, Craig, they're really worked up about this.

CRAIG. Who is?

LORIN. Pip.

CRAIG. And who?

LORIN. No one, just them.

CRAIG. Oh right. 'Them' but for one person.

LORIN. Don't do that.

CRAIG. Do what?

LORIN. It does make sense.

CRAIG. I know, I just –

LORIN. I know.

CRAIG. Okay well tell Pippa *they* can pick a takeaway.

CRAIG *is very pleased to have gotten this correct. The face of someone who has single-handedly ended transphobia.*

LORIN. Pip.

CRAIG. Christ.

LORIN. Craig.

CRAIG. Why is Pippa not okay any more?

LORIN. Because Pip is less feminine.

CRAIG *scoffs*.

Silence.

CRAIG. Okay but we can't really be expected to refer to our fully grown adult child as 'Pip'.

LORIN....

CRAIG. Pip?

LORIN....

CRAIG. Pip.

LORIN. Keep saying it, you might actually get good at it.

CRAIG. It sounds like a CBeebies character.

LORIN. Craig.

CRAIG. What?

LORIN. You still call them Pea, little petit pois. That's not exactly stately and mature.

CRAIG. What about Philip?

LORIN. Well that's a boy's name.

CRAIG. Isn't that the whole point?

LORIN. No they said they aren't either one.

CRAIG. I'm sorry – I just – This bisexuality thing is doing my nut in – I can't make sense of it.

LORIN. I don't think that's the same thing.

CRAIG. What?

LORIN. They said they're non-binary.

CRAIG. They're not bisexual?

ACT ONE 11

LORIN. No, they *are* bisexual.

CRAIG. Well that's what I said.

LORIN. No you said 'this' was about them being bisexual.

CRAIG. Yeah.

LORIN. 'This' is about them being non-binary.

CRAIG. Which is…

LORIN. A different thing to being bisexual…

Silence. A stand-off. CRAIG's *mind is working at a million miles an hour. You can almost see the steam leaking out his ears.* LORIN *is unmoving. He's so close to grasping this she knows if she moves an inch it'll be over.*

CRAIG. So they're not bisexual…

LORIN. They are – They're two different things, Craig!!

CRAIG. Oh what the fuck, Lori?? –

LORIN. They can be both at the same time!! I think.

CRAIG. See you don't even know!

LORIN. I know what my child told me. I'm trying.

CRAIG. Okay well can you and the fully grown adult named Pip *try* to pick a fucking takeaway.

LORIN. Hey.

CRAIG. Sorry.

Beat.

LORIN. I can't be the only one of us trying.

CRAIG. I am.

LORIN. The loft.

CRAIG. Not today.

LORIN. If you won't –

CRAIG. – Can't.

LORIN. If you *won't*. I'll get Pip to do it.

CRAIG. Lori –

LORIN. – Go. Protect your precious beetroot.

CRAIG. ...It's chard.

> CRAIG *picks up his gloves and goes to exit. At that moment,* PIP *comes thundering through the house in socks, joggers and a big T-shirt (the classic gender euphoria big T-shirt).*

PIP. Beep beep!

CRAIG. There's a speed limit you know.

> PIP *ignores him, they're a hurricane. Snatches up three plantains from the plate, pulls open various cupboards looking for something... something... a mug! Clearly their mug. Just like* CRAIG, PIP *has left everything open.* LORIN *slowly follows behind, shutting the doors amidst the chaos.*

LORIN. If you're putting filter on –

PIP. Instant.

LORIN. Ah.

> CRAIG *absentmindedly takes two more plantains from the plate.* LORIN *moves it gently away from him and towards herself.*

CRAIG (*mouth full*). That stuff rots you from the inside out you know – you need fresh beans.

PIP. He says atop his pile of empty Nurishment tins.

CRAIG. You think you're funny.

LORIN. They know they're funny.

CRAIG. They get that from me, you know.

PIP. Let's hope the hairline skips a generation.

> *Without skipping a beat,* PIP *jumps in to impersonate* CRAIG *as he's getting the words out himself.*

ACT ONE 13

CRAIG *and* PIP. Blasted pickney.

LORIN *isn't hiding her laughter well. One plantain left on the plate,* CRAIG *and* LORIN *stare at it, waiting, waiting, someone has to make the move.*

LORIN. Well, is anyone going to eat that last one?

CRAIG. No, you have –

PIP. Ooh, thanks, Mum.

PIP *flies in, grabs it and stuffs it in their mouth, before flying back to the coffee.* LORIN *and* CRAIG *are in complete disbelief. The silence catches* PIP's *attention, finally turning to face them.*

(*Mouth full.*) What?

LORIN. I can't believe you just did that.

PIP. What??

CRAIG. Your mum was going to have that.

PIP. Then why'd you ask if anyone wanted it?

LORIN. It's not – I was doing the polite thing. You never actually take the last one when someone asks if you want the last one.

PIP *is dumbfounded.*

CRAIG. Twenty-plus years on this earth and you haven't caught up with basic manners.

PIP. You lot are having me on. Don't say one thing if you mean the other. You two are the mannerless ones.

LORIN *and* CRAIG *are stunned.*

LORIN. They sound just like –

LORIN *erupts into roaring laughter, rolling around the room.* PIP *is left standing there, very confused.*

When – with – The After Eights! Don't you remember?

More laughter. PIP *is unimpressed.*

PIP. Well if you two are done reminiscing about the 1800s, I'm heading upstairs.

LORIN. Ooh. Burn.

PIP *stares blankly back. Exits.*

That was word for word –

Silence from CRAIG.

That was D –

CRAIG. I know.

LORIN. Honestly… Craig?

CRAIG *sits in silence for a moment. Doesn't respond, gets up to go.*

CRAIG. Look at the temperature. The whole lot'll freeze over. You two, always distracting me, wasting time.

He exits. LORIN *is left alone in the kitchen. She exhales, it heaves out all the words she didn't say. She pulls out two glasses from the back of a cupboard, stares at them. A little laugh as if she hears something from them?*

LORIN *puts the glasses back in the cupboard.* DUNCAN *swoops through and takes them from her, setting them down on the table/in a different cupboard.*

The Last Supper Part I

1993 – but we might not know it. The living room. Tables, desks and boxes from every room in the house have been brought in and pushed together into one hodgepodge table. No matter the size, shape or height, they are in. DUNCAN *holds corners of sheets, billowing them high in the air and draping them across the jumble. He is moving slowly, but not without purpose. He stops often to catch his breath.* LORIN *pokes her head through the door, holding stepladders.*

ACT ONE 15

LORIN. Duncan...

DUNCAN. My love.

LORIN. That's a lot of table space.

DUNCAN. How else am I going to fit the centrepieces on?

LORIN. How many did you invite?

DUNCAN. Six.

LORIN. And how many RSVP'd?

DUNCAN. Thirteen.

LORIN. Fantastic.

DUNCAN. Ideal. What you doing with those?

LORIN. I wanted to get everything packed and away before tonight...

DUNCAN. Craig?

LORIN. His craft calls.

DUNCAN. Is that what you call it.

DUNCAN is repeatedly trying to set the sheets, his breath barely catching, he drops to the seat behind him. LORIN, exasperated, puts down the ladders and grabs the opposite corners to help.

LORIN. Theme?

DUNCAN. Garden of Hesperides meets 'Babooshka'.

LORIN. Oh, very broad!

DUNCAN. I've been told I can be too specific.

LORIN. Shop?

DUNCAN. Already been – posh booze?

LORIN. Already hidden.

DUNCAN. Look at us.

LORIN. Look. At. Us.

CRAIG *rushes through.*

CRAIG. Hat!

LORIN. The word is hello.

DUNCAN. In the bin.

CRAIG. Funny!

DUNCAN. I'm serious. I threw it out, it was ungodly.

CRAIG. That was brand new!

DUNCAN. And now it's brand new in a Barnardo's. Here.

DUNCAN *pulls a hat out. A flat cap, almost, in the most mesmerising shade of aquatic green.*

CRAIG. I'm not wearing that.

DUNCAN. Please.

CRAIG. I love you, D, but your fashion choices can be...

DUNCAN. Mine?? Your mummy never tell you an alligator shouldn't call hog long mout? Get here.

DUNCAN *adjusts his hat on* CRAIG's *head. Meticulous. Arduous. He is creating art. Steps back, pleased with his work.*

CRAIG *turns to the mirror and tilts the hat to an angle,* DUNCAN *jumps back over and snatches the hat off his head.*

Absolutely not.

CRAIG. Trust me!

DUNCAN. Less and less every day.

CRAIG. I'm telling you, I've got style.

He pulls LORIN into his arms, a dance.

You think I snatched up the *finest* woman to ever walk this earth without *style*??

DUNCAN. Lori, bab, care to weigh in?

LORIN. No comment.

CRAIG *dips her, kisses her, then reaches back towards* DUNCAN *for the hat.* DUNCAN *reluctantly places it in his hand.* CRAIG *flips it back onto his head all while still holding* LORIN.

CRAIG. Style.

LORIN *giggles.* DUNCAN *groans.*

DUNCAN. I'm okay with you heterosexual's lifestyle choices so long as you do it in private. Children live on this street.

CRAIG *makes to leave.*

CRAIG. This looks very – What time later?

DUNCAN. Seven!

CRAIG. Seven.

DUNCAN. The last supper.

CRAIG *stops in his tracks. A beat.*

CRAIG. Don't call it that.

DUNCAN. Inner sanctum only.

CRAIG *leaves, one last kiss for* LORIN, *a nervous hug for* DUNCAN. *The landline rings,* DUNCAN *answers it; hand over the receiver, he turns to* LORIN.

It's Katya and Dianne – we need to set for fifteen.

Pip Alone

PIP *is in their room, their very messy room. They are getting ready for something, trial runs of multiple outfits are strewn across the space. They run to turn up the music from their laptop, while holding a binder out in front of them, preparing for battle.*

*

'Diary,

Today's gender aspirations are resting in the himbo department. Went jogging yesterday, saw a butch in a crop top by the park and between my asthma and their midriff I nearly passed out. So today we're trying the binder once more.

Dad still thinks that being a barista isn't a 'proper job'. Regardless, I am keeping my focus on tonight, and looking like hot shit for Maryam's birthday.'

**

With that they begin to pull it over their head. If you have ever worn a binder, you will know this is nothing to do with physical ability, this is mental, a true battle of wills. PIP *staggers around their room, arms in the air through the armholes, desperately trying to pull it down over their head and shoulders.*

PIP. Jesus Christ –

LORIN *enters.* PIP *– arms still stuck in the binder – hurls themselves over and behind the bed.*

Can you knock!

LORIN. Sorry.

PIP. Fuck, Mum!

LORIN. Sorry! Are you okay?

PIP. I'm fine.

LORIN. I can see you, you know.

PIP. Good for you.

PIP *sighs, and stands up.*

Could you help?

LORIN *is caught off-guard; she smiles, and heads to help* PIP.

(*Still tangled.*) Did you ask Dad about that garden furniture yet?

ACT ONE 19

LORIN. Why don't you ask him?

PIP. I never see him.

LORIN. You just – !

PIP. – Ouch!

LORIN. Sorry... Okay yes I can ask him. You know what he's like with 'out there' though.

PIP. It's such an ugly garden. Nothing but concrete and fake grass, I don't know why you let him do it.

LORIN. Well...

PIP. If I hadn't been a literal baby believe me I would've kicked off.

LORIN. Believe me, you kicked off plenty about everything else.

Binder on, PIP *pulls on a shirt. Bright lavender.* LORIN *adjusts their collar from behind them in the mirror. There's a brief silence,* LORIN *is looking for something to say.*

You look very pretty!

PIP *stares blankly back.*

And handsome too!

PIP. Gender euphoria, finally.

LORIN. I thought you weren't going out till later?

PIP. I'm not.

LORIN. Oh?

PIP. Just trying things on. What do you need, Mum?

LORIN. Could you help me with the loft?

This is the worst thing in the history of the entire world to PIP.

PIP. What about Dad?

LORIN *simply raises her eyebrows.*

I just got –

LORIN. Promise it won't take long, then you can go to your party.

PIP. It's not a party – it's just like everyone there at her flat.

LORIN. A bit like a party.

PIP. No it's not like a *thing* like that. It's just everyone going round there.

LORIN. Who's everyone?

PIP. Everyone. Like everyone, you know.

LORIN. Who?

PIP. Oh my god I don't know like Conor, and Erin and Bethan and Gareth – I don't know. Huw?

LORIN. I don't remember those people.

PIP. Alison will be there.

LORIN. Oh I know Alison.

PIP *smiles awkwardly. Not moving. Why is she still in here?*

So the loft? You can bring your speaker up if you want!

LORIN *starts dancing, heading out the door.* PIP *immediately turns the music off.*

Finding a Jacket

The two are in the loft, sifting through endless bags and boxes. LORIN *is forming orderly piles of what she has found,* PIP *is wearing six hats and playing with a Nintendo DS that hasn't seen the light of day since 2006, the fond tune of the Nintendogs walking music is coming from its tinny speakers.*

PIP (*shifting in disgust*). Why is the dust thick like this?

ACT ONE 21

LORIN. It's not been touched in a while...

PIP. No but isn't dust like all your dead skin and stuff, so how did it get up here?

LORIN. It's not all dead skin.

PIP puts the DS down, pulls out their phone, googles something quickly, and starts to read aloud.

PIP. Dust is made of fine particles of solid matter coming from various sources such as soil lifted by wind, volcanic eruptions, and pollution. /

LORIN. / Volcanic eruptions?

PIP. Dust in homes is composed of about twenty to fifty per cent dead skin cells.

LORIN. I don't want to think about that.

PIP. But how did it get up here then?

LORIN. I don't know – air flow or – I need you to pull that bag over – the big black one with the straps.

LORIN snatches the hats off of PIP's head and gently reaches over to shut the DS. PIP whips around with a scowl that also hasn't been seen since 2006.

PIP (*reluctantly pulling themselves up*). Looks like a body bag.

LORIN. Just pass it over please, Pippa – Pip. Pip. Sorry.

PIP. It's okay – No, it's not okay. But I get it, it's new.

LORIN. It'll be second nature soon enough.

PIP. For you.

LORIN. Your dad is working on it.

PIP (*not listening*). Mm.

LORIN. The bag, Pip.

PIP heaves over a huge black bag covered in dust, a large soft suitcase-type of bag. LORIN unzips it and immediately pulls her hands to her chest.

I had to be sure – and – oh I knew it. I knew.

PIP *is intrigued now, trying to get a glimpse of what their mum has uncovered.* LORIN *rummages around until she finds what she is looking for, a nostalgic bittersweet smile spreads across her face. She slowly pulls out the most ridiculous ski jacket you can think of. Extreme eighties. Black and white stripes with an orange flair around the base.*

PIP. Oh my god.

LORIN. Your dad's.

PIP. Shut up.

LORIN. It's true.

PIP. Liar.

LORIN. Not at all.

PIP. Oh my god.

LORIN. You should've seen him posing at the bottom of the mountain in this. Thought he was Billy Ocean.

PIP. I refuse to believe he wore this.

LORIN. Trust me, it was a struggle to get him out of it.

PIP *is in a state of absolute bewilderment.* LORIN *is looking for more.*

Here's mine.

A jacket of equal jazz. White and blue shapes, squiggles, zigzags and sprinkles cover it from arm to arm.

PIP. See, now I can see you rocking that.

LORIN. Should I be offended?

PIP. No, this jacket is incredible. It's a compliment.

LORIN. Well then thank you. I did rock it. I rocked a lot.

PIP. I have unfortunately seen photos.

LORIN. Job in a vinyl records store. Flaming red hair. Three bass guitars.

ACT ONE   23

PIP. You never said three.

LORIN *keeps digging through the bags.*

LORIN. I'm trying to see if Duncan's is here.

PIP. Dad's friend?

LORIN. Both of ours.

PIP *doesn't really respond.*

This trip was the last one we took as a group. A full group –

PIP. Yeah?

LORIN. – before he –

PIP. When did you go?

LORIN. Oh gosh, 1987? '88? He didn't – until… but you know saving took a long time and then when – After he – it all just moved very fast.

LORIN *is somehow slowing down and speeding up at the same time. Lost in thought but desperate to distract herself.*

But you know all this already. Sorry, well, you know.

PIP. Dad doesn't really talk about it.

LORIN. He doesn't.

PIP. Neither do you.

With little reaction from LORIN, PIP *loses connection and slowly reaches back for the DS.*

LORIN *isn't listening because she's found it. Out of the bag she pulls* DUNCAN's *jacket. Just as eighties as the other two, but it has this aura of confidence to it. By no means (no means at all) understated, but simply, confident. It isn't purple, pink, blue and yellow. It is violet. It is carnation. It is azure and gold in bold, strong geometric lines. Relaxed. Empowered.* Resplendent.

LORIN. That was Duncan's.

LORIN *smiles as she sees* PIP *completely enamoured by this jacket. She holds it up and out and gently shakes it at* PIP – *'try it on'.* PIP *looks wary.*

PIP. I'm sorry, who was this person? And you're sure he was friends with Dad –

LORIN *rolls her eyes and starts folding the jacket,* PIP *jumps over to stop her.*

Sorry!

PIP *gingerly slides one arm in, then another, pulling it up onto their shoulders. They look down at themselves. Trying to take it in. They reach into their pocket and pull out their phone, handing it to* LORIN.

Could you? So I can see?

LORIN *smiles and opens the camera, and holds the phone up like a mirror for* PIP *to see.*

The stage is filled with those exact same hues from the jacket, shining out of the phone, the ground, anywhere there's room for a light. PIP *is lost, stumbling. A snap. We are out of it.* LORIN *smiles with the perfect amount of warmth that only someone's mum can bring.*

She seems satisfied.

LORIN. You can keep it.

PIP *whips their head up to face* LORIN.

If you want.

Just let me tell your dad.

*

'Diary,

Warm amber buzzing. A deep... pulling hum. Soft but strong. 'Butterflies' is wrong, it's dragonflies. Dragonflies that could pull me through the roof with my chest.

Twenty-something years and I could see it all understood right there. The fog dissipated, and I saw myself with diamond-sharp clarity. I could see exactly who I was now, exactly who I'm meant to be, and exactly who I could have been ten years earlier if I had known you.

Falling through the floor, past wooden beams, through thick layers of fluffy insulation, everything taking on lavender hues. It envelops you and fills you and your cheeks are singing and your heart is surging. Lavender turned to pine turned to honey turned to rose.

Warm amber buzzing twists into sharp, cold stabs. How can I be mourning someone I never knew?

Pip x'

**

Pip and Duncan Meet

PIP *is back in their room, jacket on. They perch on the edge of their bed and stare at themselves in the mirror.*

PIP. Yeah.

They roll their shoulders back, back straight, chin lifted.

Yep.

They push their legs down to meet the floor.

That'll do it.

They stand up, look at themselves, drop into a squat. It's that vibe when there's too much going on inside of you and you have to run away from yourself without moving. They return to the mirror, cool as a cucumber, chatting up 'someone'...

'Yeah no it's a vintage piece...' 'This? Just something I sourced, yeah...' Fuck me. 'Are you cold? Here – ' FUCK –

The type of embarassment that makes you want to remove yourself from your own skin. But something catches their attention, something in the jacket? Something in the pocket? A small book stored ever so carefully in the inside pocket.

What are you?

PIP *flicks through the pages, pages thin and curled with handwriting on all sides.*

*

'02/03/93

Diary Diary Diary,

A client had an avocado shipped in today – thought he meant the fruit but no, this show-off had ordered in a whole tree. Asked me for advice on how to keep it alive – I said move it out of Walthamstow – didn't land well.

Explained to him that the flowers will have a two-day cycle if he wants it to fruit –

– First morning, flower will open and only seed-producing bits are out.

Functionally female, I told him.

– Second morning flower reopens with only the pollen-producing stamens functioning. It has changed from being female to male over the course of one night.

Told him I have a friend who does the same thing!

Looked at me like I'd shat in the petunias. Want to say fuck 'em. But I need this job.

Should shit in the petunias.

If these pages are ever published – they better be given a good name. Say there's a time when we're out of all this, a long forgotten memory that needs faded diary entries to give insight into a time we couldn't even fathom.

I do think this will be looked back on. I do. What a dream for something to be 'looked back on'. To be out of it safely enough that we can 'look back'. We'll get out of it.

Duncan's Diaries is boring. Lavender Lullabies is a bit on the gay nose but I love a gardening reference.

~~Hyacinth Hot Stuff~~. < Absolutely not.

Bought Lorin a replacement for her Take the Heat Off Me *vinyl – turns out even Boney M. is no match for a record player with a safety pin for a needle.*

I think she heard me earlier. I'm not worried about it, I know I'll have to tell them sooner or later. It's okay to keep some cries private for now though, I think.

Diary, here's to <u>all the tears I've shed in private. Freshly bottled at source.</u>

That's a good fucking title.

D x'

**

They brush through the pages, a small piece of paper falls out, a library ticket.

PIP. D. D… D! A diary? Your diary? *You* did all this plant shit too? And Dad says he learnt it himself… '*Modern Nature –* Derek Jarman', '*The Whispers – Self Titled*, cassette'. Cute. 'Ealing Library 01/1993.'

PIP *gets up, grabs their things, tucks the diary back in the jacket and begins to walk out, staring at the ticket.*

Pip and Craig

The kitchen, PIP *is pulling on their shoes, almost ready to head out, they just need a jacket – folded on the chair next to them.* CRAIG *comes in wrapped head to toe in woollen items, shaking snow off.*

CRAIG. Light frost my arse.

LORIN *comes down the stairs, more loft bags in her hands.*

Rain at twenty per cent this website says, I get out there, it's a blizzard basically. Davis with the plot next to me saved my arse with a spare poly sheet, /

PIP *is bold, brash, jacket in hand.*

PIP. / Mum! Can I ask you – so in the jacket –

LORIN *flashes a 'NOT NOW' look in* PIP's *direction, and shoves the jacket out of sight.*

CRAIG. / twenty per cent! More like a hundred per cent /

PIP. / I don't think that's what that means /

CRAIG. / Christ, Lori, you should've seen it out there /

LORIN. / Craig can I speak to you?

PIP. / Your friends. I don't want to pry I'm just feeling... a connection maybe /

CRAIG. / Tundra conditions. /

PIP. / Mum – /

LORIN. Craig? – A moment, Pip.

What about my friends? Craig –

CRAIG. Wasn't your mate going to set them up with that reception job?

PIP. Not them – D – What? Reception job?

LORIN. Okay okay let me through – Craig, don't move. Please. Pea. Don't move.

LORIN *turns to put the bags out the door.* PIP *and* CRAIG *immediately lose the animation they just had. Stood silently by each other, catching their breath, there isn't an attempt by either of them to find it again.*

PIP. I have a job.

PIP *turns to* CRAIG's *direction.* CRAIG *slightly glances, but is mostly engrossed in his phone still.*

ACT ONE 29

I think the 'twenty per cent' means a twenty-per-cent chance of rain, not that it will be at like… twenty-per-cent capacity.

CRAIG (*staring into his phone*). Hm?

PIP*'s frustration is building…*

PIP. …Did you ever have any help at the allotment –?

LORIN *re-enters*.

LORIN. Did you get Maryam a card?

PIP. Yes.

CRAIG. And now tomorrow it's saying sixty per cent! Get the bloody lifeboats out.

PIP *could scream. They compose themselves, lift up their bag, and swing on* DUNCAN*'s jacket to head out.* CRAIG *is between them and the door; he goes to move but is stopped, stunned. He can't stop staring at* PIP *in* DUNCAN*'s jacket.* LORIN *sees this and jumps in.*

LORIN. That's what I wanted to talk about – I said Pip could have it. It was in the loft.

PIP. Dad, I need to go.

CRAIG *doesn't move*.

LORIN. Doesn't it suit them?

PIP. Dad, I'm proper gunna be late.

They shift in the jacket, nervous.

Mum said I could.

PIP *looks at* LORIN.

LORIN. He'd be livid to know it was up there gathering dust.

CRAIG *whips around to face* LORIN. *That stung somewhere. A stand-off between the three of them. Eventually* CRAIG *breathes.*

CRAIG. Just – be careful with it.

PIP *rolls their eyes and exits.* LORIN *and* CRAIG *stand in silence.* LORIN *goes to head upstairs.*

You should've asked me first.

LORIN. Sorry?

CRAIG. You should have asked me, Lorin.

LORIN. I told you I was clearing out up there.

CRAIG. You should've waited for me.

LORIN. Ha! Another twenty years?

CRAIG *is silent.* LORIN *exits.*

*

'20/06/93

Diary,

What. A. Weekend.

Pride was a DREAM. Can hardly feel my feet from all the dancing, walking, marching.

And Craig.

Craig.

Angel on this earth Craig, who stuck true to his word a whole year later and stayed up till four a.m. to taxi us all around the city. He showed up in a cap, bottles of water and wet wipes in the back seats, said as the group's token straight, he was our chauffeur for the day – don't think he anticipated 'day' to mean a full twenty hours but he stuck it out.

In my garden I'd grow iris for Craig. Leaves flat as they come, but when it's in bloom? Oh baby.

D x'

**

Coming Home

Late night. LORIN *is sat up in the living room on the sofa. In front of her are the same two glasses she spoke to earlier in the day, one next to her half-drunk, the other full with a deep red drink. The TV isn't on, she's facing the window, and looks to the glasses.*

LORIN. Fine!

She picks up her phone. Puts it down. Picks it up again. Like it's a hot potato.

*

'Facebook for Apple iOS, 01/02/2013

~~Dear Elena,~~

~~Elena~~

~~Jelly!!~~

I don't know if you remember me,

It's Lorin –

~~This might be out of the blue~~

~~I'm reaching out because –~~

~~Long time no see! Are you still in Italy? Buongiorno! Haha.~~

Lorin, Jesus H Christ

Hello Elena, it's Lorin

You might not remember me, I hope you do. You came into my head the other day – do you remember those jackets?? Apparently geometrics are back in fashion. Anyway I just thought why not reach out.

Twenty-six years is a long time –

~~I'm married. To Craig!~~

I have a beautiful child. They're my absolute world. I am constantly confused and amazed and ripping my hair out.

~~I see you're married!~~

~~*Civilly partnered =*~~

I saw your special day :-)'

**

What is wrong with me?

*

'Life gets really long when you're older, doesn't it? Like you. You honestly feel like a single drop in the whole ocean of time and yet a drop that has coloured the whole thing bright orange. It stains all my clothes. I hope that makes sense.

Maybe you knew already – Duncan died.

Twenty years ago actually. Maybe that's why I'm reaching out –'

**

PIP *comes home,* LORIN *hurls her phone damn near across the room. She turns to face them, slightly blocking the glasses with her body.*

You're back early.

PIP. It's late.

LORIN. Thought you'd be later. You have a good time?

PIP. Yeah.

LORIN. Did Maryam like her present?

PIP. Who? Oh yeah.

LORIN. Make sure you drink some water before you fall asleep, okay, Pea?

PIP. Will do.

A moment.

(*Gesturing to the glasses behind* LORIN.) Is Dad up?

LORIN. Oh, no

LORIN *smiles, shifts in her seat.*

He fell asleep hours ago.

PIP. Do you think I upset him?

LORIN. No, you didn't.

PIP. He seemed pretty upset.

LORIN. Yep. But *you* didn't do anything. *I* could've maybe... Nope. No.

PIP goes to leave.

But maybe we don't have to wear that every day in front of him.

PIP. Okay.

PIP starts to perch on the edge of the sofa.

Did Dad ever like – like the whole allotment thing – did he show Duncan any of that stuff?

LORIN. Ha! Craig teach Duncan? Your dad hadn't even touched a trowel until D showed up.

PIP. So it wasn't always his thing?

LORIN. No, your dad was... He used to hole up in his room writing poetry every night.

PIP is fighting back a laugh.

He took over a lot of Duncan's jobs for him near the end, helped keep his business going. Think he caught the love of it then.

PIP. And Duncan...

LORIN. Taught him everything he knows.

PIP. Was he...?

LORIN. What?

PIP waits, waits, offering an opportunity to LORIN. Their mum isn't picking it up. They hold their arms out, gesturing to the jacket, themselves, nothing. They drop it, frustrated.

PIP. And so Dad and the gardening now, it's for Duncan?

LORIN. For?

PIP. Like, memory stuff.

LORIN *shrugs, almost laughs.*

LORIN. That concrete monstrosity of a back garden, plus the allotment none of us are allowed to touch? Feels more male-ego hobby than 'in memoriam'.

PIP. Okay.

LORIN. It might be though.

PIP. Maybe.

LORIN. Why'd you ask?

PIP (*pulling the jacket tighter over their shoulders*). I know you gave it to me, but –

LORIN. – I'm glad you're wearing it, Pip.

PIP. Are you sure?

LORIN. I miss him, and I want him back. It's nice to see him back.

PIP *fumbles with the zip. Big.*

PIP. Okay. I'm after that water. Night.

LORIN. Night.

PIP. Also, we're circling back to that poetry revelation in the morning.

We're Going to Live Forever

1992. Three a.m.?? Four a.m.? Clocks aren't really making sense right now. CRAIG *and* DUNCAN *get home from EUROPRIDE 1992. Each one somehow drunker than the other. A cluster of giggles and dances as they unlock the door and creep inside.*

CRAIG. Two *hundred* pounds!!

DUNCAN. It was twenty quid, bab.

CRAIG. For a taxi.

DUNCAN. Next year you be designated driver then.

CRAIG. You want me to take my car *south of the river*?

DUNCAN *waits.*

Okay fine.

DUNCAN. Promise?

CRAIG. *Promise.*

DUNCAN. Shh!

CRAIG. Shhh!! Shh.

DUNCAN. SHHHH!!

A quick beep-beep from outside. DUNCAN *leans out the window and waves.*

BYEE, GUYS!!

CRAIG. What happened to shh?

DUNCAN. Don't know her. Are you hot? It's hot.

CRAIG. I'm boiling. And also hot.

CRAIG *strikes a pose.* DUNCAN *leans back out the window.*

DUNCAN. *I'm so hot!!*

CRAIG. Neighbours.

DUNCAN. That racist old biddie downstairs??

CRAIG. Margaret.

DUNCAN. Well if she's homophobic too maybe she'll finally keel over.

CRAIG. She actually isn't. Told me she loves how tidy you all are.

DUNCAN. Oh. Well I'm evening it out then.

DUNCAN *returns to waving out the window.*

DID YOU HEAR ME, LONDON?? I SAID I'M SO HOT!!

CRAIG *stumbles to join him.*

CRAIG. A MI FI TELL YU – 1992 YEAR OF THE ABSOLUTE FITTESTFITBOYS TO EVER LIVE.

DUNCAN. Craig Angelique Forester –

CRAIG. It's Angelo –

DUNCAN. Look at you.

CRAIG *is suddenly deeply serious.*

CRAIG. I'm going to live forever, mate.

DUNCAN. Don't I know it.

CRAIG. They'll make a museum for me.

DUNCAN. A museum!

CRAIG. All my stuff, laid out for the tourists. They'd want for nothing.

DUNCAN. How'd they get your stuff if you're living forever?

CRAIG. Donations. It's called being philanthropic.

DUNCAN. What a night.

CRAIG. What a night! That wasn't regular old Pride. /

DUNCAN. / Regular old?

CRAIG. / In order: eighty-eight, ninety-one,

DUNCAN. / Oh?

CRAIG. / BACK TO eighty-nine *THEN* 1992 now takes number-one spot.

DUNCAN. One more and you get a free CD.

CRAIG. EUROPRIDE!

DUNCAN. EUROPRIDE! Plus first time we've had a 'people of colour' tent /

CRAIG. / Is that why everyone was smiling at us?

DUNCAN *reads from his magazine.*

DUNCAN. 'After *years* of non-participation of lesbians and gay men of colour in the festival we can expect to see up to *one thousand* Black lesbians, gay men and bisexuals coming to celebrate in the middle of South London.'

CRAIG. Where'd you get that?

DUNCAN. A guy was flogging them.

CRAIG. You said you had no money!

DUNCAN. Yeah, now I don't, bab.

The phone rings. CRAIG *turns to answer it.*

CRAIG. Hello? Who? No this is Craig. Who?? Miguel??

DUNCAN. – Oh give me that it's for me. Olá!!

CRAIG. For you? D? Have you been giving out my phone number as yours?

DUNCAN. Well I'm not going to let strange men know my area code, am I? (*Back to the phone.*) I was SO cute I know!!

CRAIG. D –

He snatches the phone and puts it back on the receiver.

DUNCAN. Hey! Me and Michael were having an important conversation.

CRAIG. Miguel.

DUNCAN. What are you, his husband?

CRAIG *shoots a finger gun at* DUNCAN.

CRAIG. EUROPRIDE.

Hurricane Pip Spotted Off Shore

PIP *is standing a little taller. Something about them… lighter.*

*

'Dear Diary,

D, I don't know how you found so much room in this city. Every day new flats soar up around us and shroud what little green

*I can find in shadow. Today, your record recommendation was
'Sign o' the Times' – Prince. Type of song got me walking a little
slower, but a little stronger.*

*I see your Prince, and raise you one Janelle Monáe. Mentor,
mentee – trying not to make too many obvious comparisons.*

*There is a version of my father in your words that I do not
recognise. You've made complete strangers of my parents. It's
fucked, D.*

What did you have that brought such vibrancy out of him?

Or what is it that I lack?

*Sometimes outside of the front gardens lining my walks, I see
the tiniest violas, pansies, pushing cracks through paving
stones.*

*Again, obvious comparisons, but I'd like to crack some paving
stones I think.*

– ~~Pip~~

– P x'

**

DUNCAN *enters, sets up himself on a garden chair with sunnies
and SPF, as* PIP *brushes through his diary and reads aloud.*

*

'27/06/1993

Diary,

*I'm beginning to grow thorny in my lungs. I feel them catching
more and more.*

Rang Mummy. She still refuses to say AIDS out loud but –

*She told me to come home. I said I am home. She said to look
after Craig. I said I am. She said she would write to Lady Di for
me. Again.*

D x'

**

Craig and Duncan Garden

1993. A gardening job. DUNCAN *is sitting in a camping chair, sunglasses on, face back, a parasol popped to his left.* CRAIG *enters with three great hulking bags of top soil.*

DUNCAN. I'm getting my tan up.

CRAIG. You're Black, Duncan.

DUNCAN. And I'd like to stay that way, thank you very much.

DUNCAN *waves his hand loosely.*

Just drop them down over there.

CRAIG. Here?

DUNCAN (*very much not looking*). Yeah just wherever.

CRAIG *drops the bags right on the flowers.* DUNCAN *lifts his glasses.*

Not there!! Jesus, Craig.

CRAIG. You said wherever!

DUNCAN. Have you no sense? No decorum?

CRAIG. I skipped the bit when they were giving those out – I was too busy getting my winning smile.

A look from DUNCAN *and* CRAIG *quickly moves the bags.*

What's next?

DUNCAN *scooches his chair forwards.*

DUNCAN. These hyacinths – bulbs. Take this. See, we're going to bury them point-up, ten centimetres down.

CRAIG *grabs one and drops it in a hole point-down.*

Point-up.

CRAIG. Which end is the point?

DUNCAN. The pointy end.

CRAIG. Thanks.

DUNCAN *gently rotates the bulb and hands it back to* CRAIG.

Okay.

CRAIG *immediately starts going, a slow start tumbles into him racing through it. Bulbs are left tops-out all over the place.* DUNCAN *looks on in horror.*

DUNCAN. Okay – okay – easy, easy!! Cyan bury a man an lef out him foot?

CRAIG. We've got a lot to do, you said.

DUNCAN. And we'll get it done. We have time.

Silence. Their eyes don't meet.

We have time today.

CRAIG. Yes.

DUNCAN. But I won't have a job tomorrow if you don't fix those bulbs.

CRAIG. Okay.

DUNCAN. Take it slow. Every extra second of effort you put in is another flower on that bulb and another penny in my tip jar.

CRAIG *very dramatically takes his time.* DUNCAN *leans back in his chair and turns the radio up, the rhythm begins to set in as* CRAIG *fixes each bulb, clearly beginning to enjoy himself.*

Now try doing four, five at a time, then cover them up. Lets you see what you're doing better.

CRAIG *lines them up, drops them in, fills the holes. It's the perfect rhythm. Soon half the bed is done.*

CRAIG. Three, four, five. In. One, two, three, four, five. In. One, two, three, four –

DUNCAN. See, you're not just a pretty face.

CRAIG. And when do we get to see these famous flowers?

DUNCAN. *Hyacinths* – named after a very famous gay lover, don't you know!

CRAIG. Of yours?

DUNCAN. Of Apollo.

CRAIG. Is he the one who left that bottle of Rush on the floor of my car?

DUNCAN. The ancient Greek god of music. The sun. Arts.

CRAIG. Ah.

DUNCAN. They'll flower at the end of the year.

CRAIG. End of the year?!

DUNCAN. They're bulbs, bab!

CRAIG. Lorin's tomatoes sprouted in a week.

DUNCAN (*holding up a bulb*). Little powerhouses of hibernating energy. When they do pop up they'll stand stronger and brighter than any flower out here.

CRAIG. Probably because it'll be December.

DUNCAN. November. Takes a bulb to make it through that.

CRAIG. I'll be a dad before these bloody flowers show up.

DUNCAN. You will.

CRAIG. There's something in that...

He pulls out his notebook.

'I'll be a dad before these flowers show up... Lorin's belly a bulb...'

DUNCAN. Dear god. Come on. Back to it, Langston.

CRAIG. Sorry.

DUNCAN. No poetry at my funeral by the way.

CRAIG. We don't – Let's just –

DUNCAN. I'm serious.

CRAIG. That's not what –

DUNCAN. What then?

CRAIG. Talking like – We don't know what time will bring, okay.

DUNCAN (*under his breath*). I've got a clue.

CRAIG. I heard that.

> DUNCAN *blows him a kiss.* CRAIG *turns away and back to the bulbs.*

DUNCAN. Hey! I'm not – I'm not like giving up. Just – Keep it light. Have some humour in it.

CRAIG. Humour?

DUNCAN. Yeah.

CRAIG. I don't have any humour in it, D.

DUNCAN. Well I need you to.

CRAIG. I don't have that in me.

DUNCAN. Find it.

> CRAIG *goes back to the bulbs. He can't find the rhythm. Frustrated, he throws them down into the earth.*

I said point-up.

CRAIG. Christ, Duncan!

DUNCAN. Not the government name.

CRAIG. All I have is scared. Scared. That's all I have. And it's all I'll ever have until this is fixed.

Beat.

DUNCAN. You're allowed to be scared.

CRAIG. I'm not.

DUNCAN. Because it won't be fixed, bab.

> CRAIG *can't hear this.*

CRAIG. How many more bulbs?

DUNCAN. No.

CRAIG. D.

DUNCAN. I could get hit by a car tomorrow, we don't know. I need you to know my funeral plans.

CRAIG huffs. Pinches his brow.

CRAIG. I already know your funeral plans.

DUNCAN. What?

CRAIG. You told me them.

DUNCAN. When?

CRAIG. Six years ago. The morning after your twenty-fifth. I seem to remember your head resting on the edge of a toilet seat at the time.

DUNCAN. Christ.

CRAIG flops his head across DUNCAN's lap, mimicking him perfectly,

CRAIG. 'I'm not making it out of this one, Craig. Just respect my last wishes.'

DUNCAN. To this day I don't know how I survived.

CRAIG. No black, no lilies,

BOTH. No cider.

DUNCAN. Bang on.

CRAIG. And now, no poetry. Any other funeral classics you want to ban? No crying?

DUNCAN. You better fucking cry.

CRAIG. Songs are allowed?

DUNCAN. Encouraged. Only Lorin is allowed to touch the mix though.

Horrified, CRAIG *completely stops what he's doing.*

Back to the hyacinths!

CRAIG. Oh come on.

DUNCAN. My last wish.

CRAIG. Can I sing?

DUNCAN. Give it a go and I'm jumping out of the coffin and bringing you down with me.

CRAIG *looks at the radio, turns it up. He starts singing. It's 'Silly Games' by Janet Kay, and he does* not *have the range.*

CRAIG *sings the first line of the third verse.*

Craig –

CRAIG *continues to sing the next line.*

I swear –

CRAIG *sings the next two lines.*

He points an imaginary microphone DUNCAN*'s way.* DUNCAN *finally gives in and they sing the final two lines of the verse together.*

DUNCAN *grabs a rake off the floor, a standing mic in the arms of Janet Kay herself.* CRAIG *meanwhile has grabbed two soil bags, holding them either side of him. He two-steps as he and the bags become the perfect backing singers – à la* Dreamgirls.

DUNCAN *heads into the pre-chorus.*

CRAIG *joins him for the third line and then takes a daring solo on the fourth.* DUNCAN *takes the next line. And then they both launch into the chorus.*

DUNCAN *starts coughing, still laughing, then the laughing stops but the coughing continues. He stumbles back over his chair and* CRAIG *grabs him.*

CRAIG. D? D? Hey, look at me.

DUNCAN*'s coughing slows as he manages to catch his breath. It is laboured and wheezing.*

Come on, mate, inside you go, I've got this.

DUNCAN. It's cold out here, is all.

CRAIG. D –

DUNCAN (*a snap, acid*). It's fucking freezing, Craig.

CRAIG. ...Baltic.

> CRAIG *picks up the suncream, sunglasses, pops down the parasol, and watches* DUNCAN *head inside.*

Pip and Craig I

The allotment. CRAIG *is kneeling on a foam knee rest, meticulously counting seeds in his palm and placing them into nursery trays.* PIP *approaches from behind, proudly sporting* DUNCAN*'s jacket.*

CRAIG. Three, four, five. In. One, two, three, four, five. In. One, two – no two, three, four –

PIP. What's on the agenda today?

CRAIG (*startled*). Christ, Pea. Is everything alright? Why are you here?

PIP. Nice to see you too.

CRAIG. Did I forget something?

PIP. No I just – I just wanted to hang out.

CRAIG. Oh.

PIP. Yeah.

CRAIG. Okay.

PIP. I was going to ask for a lift but you were gone already so – and then I realised I didn't actually know which spot was yours so I've just been wandering around for forty minutes. Someone down in the back corner is definitely burning a body –

CRAIG. Careful, Pea!

PIP. What?

CRAIG. Please just, watch where you're standing.

PIP. You need to get a path in.

CRAIG. It's a vegetable patch.

PIP. This is fully a death trap, Dad. People could trip over like, everything here. Look at these wires –

PIP *reaches down to twang on some cords stretched out across the plant beds.*

CRAIG. Easy! Just try not to mess with stuff.

PIP. Sorry.

CRAIG. No, it's fine – just – there.

CRAIG *gestures to a fold-out camping chair in the back corner of the plot.* PIP *steps over the twine and sits down in it. It's just far enough away to be extremely awkward. They tuck their knees up onto it and watch their dad go back to counting seeds.*

PIP. What're you planting?

CRAIG. Aubergines. Trying to.

PIP. You ever thought about flowers in here?

They try to come closer.

CRAIG. Careful, Pip. Look – Don't get any dirt on that jacket while it's out.

PIP. Mum did say I could keep it.

Silence.

I uh – did some reading about 'queer ecology'. It's like this area of study that brings together queer theory and eco-criticism. And there's a lot about plant life in there.

CRAIG *is not responding.*

It's about how all of science and academia is looked at through this heteronormative lens. So if we share marginalised perspectives and support more diverse representations in areas like botany, we can learn so much more. Like so many plants are like, queer.

CRAIG. I'm trying to count.

PIP. Like hyacinths, named after this guy – called Hyacinth – and he was Apollo's lover.

CRAIG *has stopped, just for a moment. He catches himself.*

Very cute, very gay. And he was so hot the wind got jealous and knocked him out with a discus, and so Apollo made the flowers out of his dead body.

CRAIG. Okay.

PIP. So like, without the gays we wouldn't have hyacinths. /

CRAIG. I thought we couldn't say 'the gays' any more /

PIP. And there's also stuff like yew trees! They can do this incredible thing where like they can just pick bits of their branches to be seed-producing, and bits to be pollen-producing, all on the same tree. Just being completely sex-fluid all in one organism. And they can change it around all the time.

CRAIG. Like in pumpkin plants there are separate male flowers and female flowers –

PIP. Seed-producing and pollen-producing.

CRAIG. Excuse me?

PIP. So! A lot of it is about how labelling things male and female doesn't actually make much sense, and is kind of forcing a binary onto things that exist outside of it.

CRAIG. And where did you read this?

PIP. I saw your jacket up there too – very eighties.

CRAIG. Hm.

PIP. Looked like a fun holiday, from the clothes.

CRAIG. It was.

PIP. Do you have any photos?

CRAIG. Your mum does, maybe.

PIP. Would be cool to see all three of you.

CRAIG. I don't think there's any like that.

PIP. Was he a good skier?

CRAIG. Who?

PIP. Duncan.

CRAIG. Terrible. Like a baby giraffe. Keep your feet off the twine.

PIP. Did he have a partner? Or a boyf–

CRAIG. The twine, Pip.

PIP. Sorry.

CRAIG. I'm a bit – I'm busy here. You could have a think about what we should start planting in March, if you'd like? /

PIP. / I just want to know a little about –

CRAIG. I have other friends you know, why don't you ask about them?

PIP. They're not – well – as far as I know…

CRAIG. What?

PIP. Just – trying to keep queer histories going.

Silence.

CRAIG. Do you want to help transplant the beetroot seedlings?

PIP *hesitates*.

Do you want to help or not?

PIP. Yes.

CRAIG. I thought you said you were interested in this stuff.

PIP. I am.

CRAIG. Then come see these shoots.

> PIP *gets up, defeated, steps over the twine.*

And take that jacket off before you get it dirty.

Talking Points

LORIN *is dragging the last of the bags from the loft to go to the charity shop, far too many for one person.* CRAIG *and* PIP *enter with shoes covered in mud and walk straight past* LORIN *to the table.* CRAIG *is rambling on about something, and we can feel it's probably been going on for the past hour at least.*

CRAIG. And I know you're excited about all this, I reckon it would be a good idea to get some basics down first so you really know what you're talking about.

PIP. I do know what I'm –

CRAIG. I know I know of course you know all that new stuff, but you know you've got to know the basics. The roots.

PIP. Okay.

CRAIG. The roots.

PIP. I heard you.

CRAIG. No one appreciates true humour in this house.

PIP (*deflated*). Sorry.

> *They head to go upstairs.*

LORIN (*to* PIP). Shoes!

> PIP *stops, slumps to the floor and starts pulling their shoes off in the middle of the room.*

Did you have a good time?

CRAIG. Did you hear me?

LORIN. The roots. Yes. Very funny.

CRAIG. It's a lonely life being the only comedian here.

LORIN (*mouthing to* CRAIG). Are they okay?

CRAIG (*loudly*). I'll tell you what, they actually know some stuff – I'm not sure of all of it, bit complicated but I reckon if they get on a horticulture course they'd learn some really useful basics.

PIP. I was talking about decolonising the way we look at the natural world – a course in a Western academic institution isn't going to do that.

CRAIG (*lost in his phone*). There's a university in Kent that does one!

LORIN *and* PIP *share an exhausted look before* LORIN *begins to usher* CRAIG *upstairs; clearly this is going nowhere helpful.*

LORIN. Come on, into the shower please. You two have trailed enough mud through this house.

CRAIG *leaves,* LORIN *turns to* PIP.

What happened to helping me? I told you, baby steps with your dad. You wore that to drop in on him?

PIP. So Duncan was gay.

LORIN *is stunned. She waits.* PIP *waits.* LORIN *smiles.*

LORIN. And the horticulture course?

PIP. Mum.

LORIN. I'm sure you already knew.

PIP *does not budge.*

Okay maybe we didn't parade it around, but give us some grace here, Pea.

PIP *shrugs.*

Did your dad tell you?

PIP. No. Can you talk to him?

LORIN. About what?

ACT ONE 51

PIP. Like I want us to be like – like we don't talk about anything serious and I – just closer, I guess.

LORIN. You want me to talk to him for you, about the two of you being closer?

PIP. Yes. No, I – I just –There's no way he was always like this –

PIP *reluctantly begins to pull out the diary, but stops as* CRAIG *strolls back in, still covered in plant matter, this time holding a towel as well as his phone. The towel is now also covered in said plant matter.*

CRAIG. So I don't know about that Kent one actually, but they do one in Newcastle – bit far but it leads to an internship at Kew.

PIP *makes a face at* LORIN, *wide-eyed 'HELP!' as they get up and head upstairs.* CRAIG *lost in his phone is none the wiser that* PIP *has left the room.*

Oh no, maybe that's Manchester.

LORIN. Is this really important right now?

CRAIG. Hm? (*Looking around.*) Oh.

LORIN. I'm not entirely sure this is what Pip was getting at. Doing a whole degree.

CRAIG. It's just something to get them back up and out there.

LORIN. I think they were looking at it as something to do with you.

CRAIG. Need to know the foundations first though –

LORIN. You looked after Duncan's garden for two weeks and tried to set up an aquaponics farm.

CRAIG *looks at* LORIN, *moves on.*

CRAIG. It's just all this bisexual stuff again, I don't get how it can apply to plants. Is growing tomatoes heteronormative now?

LORIN. Big word.

CRAIG. I was paying attention.

LORIN. We could always just go and ask them?

CRAIG. It just seems to me like this is another checkbox on the long list of things that we have failed at because we haven't denounced our birth certificates.

LORIN. You need to start listening to them, Craig.

CRAIG. I'm not saying it's wrong – I'm not. I'm not. I love them and this world is fucked up for people like – I know that. I'm just saying –

LORIN. Don't you think they look taller?

CRAIG. What?

LORIN. *Don't you think they look taller?* They'll outgrow us, Craig. Look up.

*

'*D,*

It's all mulch. Well, I'd like it to all be mulch. Compost and litter and substrate and <u>mulch</u>.

I dream of mulch but wake in a pot. Terracotta. Rootbound. I can't reach anything outside it.

Black. And Queer. With Your Whole Entire Body.

The obvious part of this is that no matter how safe it now feels with age. It did not feel safe then.

There is no world where you were resurrected for me in sinew and tendon, just because they said your name.

But

Knowing you existed

Knowing you thrived

Who am I, then?

How <u>easy</u> is it all then?

– P x'

**

A Good Ally

LORIN *and* CRAIG*'s bedroom.* PIP *is neck-deep in* CRAIG*'s wardrobe, scouring through shirts and blazers and T-shirts. They pull several from hangers and hold them up against themselves in the mirror, working on different outfits and combinations.*

PIP. This is maybe the ugliest shirt I've ever seen. It's perfect.

CRAIG. Can I help you?

PIP. As part of my genderless journey I am taking on the important task of reclaiming garish shirts from old men.

CRAIG. Oh fantastic.

PIP. Can I wear this?

CRAIG. Where you off to?

PIP. Gig.

CRAIG. It looks alright on you.

PIP *immediately takes it off.*

Who's playing?

PIP. Friend's band – hey do you have any blazers that aren't brown?

CRAIG. Yes, you can look through my wardrobe. Thanks for asking.

CRAIG *is awkwardly standing, preparing the words.*

So all your friends, they're cool with you being non-binary?

PIP. ...Well they wouldn't be my friends if they weren't.

CRAIG. Yeah of course. Just – you know just gotta check. People can be different than you expect sometimes, is all I mean.

PIP. They're all good.

CRAIG. That's good.

PIP. Yeah. (*A pause.*) Thanks for asking though.

CRAIG. Dad duties. I wore that on your mum and I's first wedding anniversary. We went to this spoken-word night –

PIP. – Oh were you performing?

CRAIG. – Hm?

PIP. Nothing.

PIP *returns to holding clothes up against themselves in the mirror.*

CRAIG. Things are new to me, when I thought we were done with 'new'. I would like to do right by you, Pea. You know that, yeah? I don't get it, but I want to be an 'ally' or whatever you lot call it.

PIP. Okay.

CRAIG. Okay.

PIP. Thanks.

CRAIG. You're welcome, Pea. Pip.

CRAIG *goes for a hug, handshake, hug. Settles on boys'-style dab. It's awkward yet affirming for them both. He and* PIP *clear their throats in panic and go back to the wardrobe.*

PIP. Being a good ally means letting your kid wear your clothes to concerts.

CRAIG. Well then I think that blazer you're eyeing up is where my allyship ends.

PIP *pulls out the blazer, classic, simple, very expensive...*

No way.

PIP. Please!

CRAIG. No!

ACT ONE 55

PIP. Letting this blazer live in this world without at least once being paired with its own bodyweight of gold jewellery should be a criminal offence.

CRAIG. Pea!

PIP. Please!

CRAIG. Put it back.

PIP. 'Supportive parent points' opportunity /

CRAIG. My god. /

PIP. And you're just going to let it go?

CRAIG. Seriously.

PIP. I'll even get it dry-cleaned!

CRAIG. ...Promise?

PIP. Yeah I just need to borrow twenty quid first.

CRAIG *makes a lunge for the hanger, but* PIP *leaps up and over the bed with it, the grace of someone attempting 100m hurdles for the very first time. It is pure mania.*

Please!

CRAIG. Moon run faas but day catch im eventually!

PIP. It's allyship time!

CRAIG. Back!

PIP. Come on!! What happened to the Craig who drove Duncan around until four a.m. on Pride?! He knew how to support the queers!

PIP *keeps running but* CRAIG *has stopped.* PIP *slows down to standing in the centre of the bed.*

CRAIG. What?

PIP. Just that – You know it's just one night out...

CRAIG. How do you know about that?

PIP. I don't have to wear this, if it's too much.

CRAIG. Did your mum tell you?

PIP. I read it.

CRAIG. What?

PIP. I read it. There was a book in D's jacket.

CRAIG. 'D's'?

PIP *is silent.*

Where is it now?

PIP. In the jacket.

CRAIG *leaves.* PIP *is left standing on the bed.* CRAIG *comes back in, diary in one hand, jacket in the other. He is upset, clearly.*

CRAIG. Sit down.

PIP *sits.*

I understand why you'd read this, if you found it.
I understand that part. But I don't – what I don't get is…
This is one thing – (*He holds up the jacket.*) but this – (*He raises the diary.*) This is a territory you do not cross, Pip. There's respect – there has to be respect, when it comes to these things. Dealing with people who have…

I'm searching for the words here that won't make this worse.

PIP. You didn't even tell me he was gay. How he died. Do you know how significant that is –

CRAIG. That's nothing to do with – Pip. You – You weren't there. The second you knew what this was you should've given it back to me.

PIP. Given it *back*?

CRAIG. Yes. It's not yours –

PIP. It's not yours either.

CRAIG *stops himself from blowing up. Exhales. Heads over to his wardrobe where he pushes the diary into the back of a drawer – it's very specific where he places it, like he knew where it should go.* PIP *watches it all.*

PIP *leaves.* CRAIG *stands up, stops. Waits. He goes back to the drawer and pulls out the diary he just put in. He looks around. Waits agonisingly long with the book. Pulls it open to a random page, looking as if one wrong move it could explode.*

*

'*18/07/1993*

Diary,

Booked a surprise trip. Scotland. The three of us. Would've been a nice surprise for them. Big witchy yew tree for Lorin, a lot of whisky for Craig.

Craig says I'm 'not strong enough right this moment. Give it a few months'.

A few months.

I threw it all back in their faces, didn't I? ~~Unmoving ungrateful flamingo-legged~~ *And I called him all that, to his face. He gave it just as good back.*

When will that boy get a fucking grip and learn to loosen his shoulders??

Things that don't bend have a tendency to end up snapping.

And after all that vitriol I threw their way, you know what they did?'

**

CRAIG *quickly shuts the book. A moment. The tiniest smile. Of course. He dares to open it once more.*

*

'They asked me to move in with them.

I think I will. I need the help.

I know he wants to let go. I just don't think he even tries.

– D x'

**

CRAIG *shuts the book again. No more. He's done. He puts it away, wipes his face. Done.*

Conversations in Bed

Lorin and Craig's bedroom, the middle of the night, maybe later. Probably later. They are both in bed, LORIN *fast asleep,* CRAIG *staring at the ceiling or the wall or both.*

CRAIG. Do you think I 'try'?

LORIN *pulls the duvet tighter over her face.*

Lori?

LORIN. What?

CRAIG. Do you think I try.

LORIN. Try what?

CRAIG. In general.

LORIN. With other people?

CRAIG. Well –

LORIN. No. I think you tell them you are, but you aren't.

CRAIG. I am.

LORIN. Why did you ask me if that's going to be the answer?

CRAIG. I think I am.

LORIN. Well then carry on.

LORIN *returns to the duvet.*

CRAIG. I don't, do I?

LORIN. What time is it?

CRAIG. Too late.

LORIN. Too early.

A moment.

CRAIG. If we have a barbecue or something –

LORIN. What – Craig – When have we ever had a barbecue?

CRAIG. Summers are getting warmer.

LORIN. That concrete is too hot to sit on when it's sunny.

CRAIG. Okay well let's see how it goes.

LORIN. Is that all?

CRAIG. Yes. Do you think I try with you?

LORIN. If you have to ask.

LORIN turns to face him.

Are we doing this?

CRAIG. Honesty.

LORIN. …Honesty. I think you act as though you're the glue holding us together /

CRAIG. / Trying to.

LORIN. And it's actually me.

CRAIG. Oh.

LORIN. And it's exhausting.

CRAIG. Oh.

LORIN. It's fucking exhausting, Craig.

CRAIG. Oh.

They lay in silence for a moment. A while.

Honesty?

LORIN. Honesty! Listen.

CRAIG. ...I knew that.

LORIN. Hm.

CRAIG. And I hoped you'd lie. Just now.

LORIN. I think I want to be done with that.

CRAIG. The glue?

LORIN. The lying.

CRAIG. Right. Is there anything else you lie about?

LORIN. I don't know. I'll think on it.

Beat.

I think about him so much. And I keep it in.

CRAIG. Why?

LORIN. For you!

CRAIG. It's just all so... all at once. The jacket –

LORIN. It's just a fucking jacket. If we're in our fifties and we're not allowed to reminisce then god help us both.

CRAIG *is giving nothing.*

I'd like to talk to my child about the man that would've helped raise them.

CRAIG. I never said you couldn't talk to Pip –

LORIN *bursts out into the biggest scoff the world has ever known.* CRAIG *is quiet.*

They're callous with it. I don't know how to try with them.

LORIN. Just – step into their world.

CRAIG. How?

LORIN *looks at* CRAIG *expectantly.*

You're right.

Lights flick on.

How do I get on that Trainlines app you use?

LORIN. Fucking hell!

CRAIG. Sorry.

LORIN. Now?!

CRAIG. Sorry, yes, tomorrow. I read in D– ...did do a google earlier on this tree in Scotland –

LORIN. You want some honesty right now?

CRAIG *crawls back into bed, arms around* LORIN.

CRAIG. Sorry.

Do you remember how much Duncan loved Pip?

A moment. LORIN *is stunned. One wrong move and this bursts.*

LORIN. Of course I do.

CRAIG. From the second they were born.

Beat.

That's something I think about a lot.

LORIN. I do too.

CRAIG *kisses the side of* LORIN*'s head, turns the lights off, and returns to sleep.*

Small Baby

Immediately, DUNCAN *walks past the open door. 1993. He peers through the doorway to the crib at the base of their bed, smiling at a teeny tiny Pip as their parents (finally) get a moment's sleep.*

DUNCAN. You are so small.

It's true.

The tiniest.

Smallest.

Small baby.

(*Baby voice*.) Yes!

You are so small and yet you made your mummy and daddy age forty years in four days.

Yes!

Aren't you just the littlest teeniest devil spawn!

Me and you both, hey.

Here's something.

Your mummy's midwife was a lesbian.

Mm-hmm.

That's the first thing they told me. As if we'd be related or something.

But what's important there actually is –

the first hands to ever touch you were *gay*.

That means we own you.

Mm-hmm.

Claimed.

I didn't think this day would come.

Who knows what other days will come now…

If this one did.

Maybe.

Maybe not.

Maybe.

Can I be candid with you, small baby?

I have often felt alone.

I've heard I can be… abrasive?

ACT ONE 63

I do not feel alone with you.

Do what you love.

And don't stand under ladders.

Forget that last part. Well don't.

It's just less important.

This was meant to be a memorable interaction.

You're four days old, what are you going to remember?

Well, one can hope.

He thinks, and then quickly.

The best Spudulike topping is plain cheese. I stand by it. You will too.

Prince is a better guitarist than George Harrsion, don't listen to your mother.

The second you get your ID, we're hitting the club. The Vox. You and me. Okay.

Okay.

I love you, small baby.

Keep it down tonight, yeah?

How am I meant to go peacefully in my sleep if you keep screaming at three a.m.?

Well…

Once again, forget that last part.

I love you.

Night night.

As DUNCAN *makes to leave,* CRAIG *turns over to face him, whispers, barely awake.*

CRAIG. You're not taking my newborn child to The Vox.

DUNCAN. *I said* when the ID came in. Seventeen years and three hundred and sixty-one days to practise being cool.

CRAIG. You okay?

DUNCAN. Just going for a piss. Christ. You can help if you like? Or have you changed enough nappies today?

CRAIG. Potentially.

DUNCAN. I'm afraid the adult ones don't have ducks on them.

CRAIG (*going to sit up*). Are you –

DUNCAN. I'm fine.

CRAIG. Okay.

DUNCAN. Back to bed.

CRAIG. Okay.

DUNCAN. Love you.

CRAIG. Love you.

DUNCAN. I was speaking to the baby, you massive queer.

Alone Again

PIP *is sat in their room, scribbling in their diary.*

*

'*D,*

There's a version of my parents that I genuinely think I could meet at a party and not want to die. Like, they were alright? They were effervescent? And crawling? And bold and brash and full and I don't want to let that go.

I feel like you wrote those words for me, and they shouldn't be hidden away.

There's internships at Kew. I was considering them but I think it would make my dad think he was right – absolutely not.'

**

CRAIG *bursts in.* PIP *is horrified.*

CRAIG. Do you want to go to Scotland?

PIP. Dad!

CRAIG. Do you want to go to Scotland?

PIP. Is that a threat?

> LORIN *appears behind him.*

LORIN. I did tell him to knock first.

> CRAIG *starts blasting 'Sweet Dreams' by Eurythmics from his phone, and dancing around the room. It is premium dad dancing. Artisanal.*

PIP. What is happening?

LORIN. Your dad has a holiday plan.

> CRAIG *is still going.*

At least that's what he was meant to be explaining to you.

PIP. Are we meant to infer it through dance?

LORIN. Just let him get it out of his system.

> CRAIG *finally slows.*

CRAIG. Annie Lennox is Scottish!

LORIN. Ah.

PIP. Please someone just say what's going on.

LORIN. Craig?

CRAIG. What?

LORIN. It's your plan.

CRAIG. I don't know if it's *my* plan... You can say it if you want.

LORIN. My god, the pair of you.

> PIP *and* CRAIG *look, confused, at* LORIN. LORIN *stands firm.*

PIP. So...

CRAIG. The yew trees! There's one in Scotland, the Fortingall Yew it's called. Supposedly it's over five thousand years old.

PIP. Oh, cool.

CRAIG. More than cool! Everybody shut up. Sorry. No. Everybody listen. Who's yelling?

PIP. You're yelling.

CRAIG. Oh – well, the tree! They think it's doing the sex-change thing.

PIP *raises their eyebrows.*

Gender... change... It transitioned to um...

PIP. No, no, Dad, you were right I wasn't –

CRAIG. It's got berries! They think. On one bit it looks like. Oldest tree in Britain and it's doing a sex-change!

PIP *is beaming.*

Anyway. Only if you're interested.

PIP. No, I am!

CRAIG. Yeah?

PIP. Yeah!

CRAIG. I'm booking trains! Lorin, where's your railcard?

CRAIG *storms out with as much gusto as he entered with.*

PIP. Do we have any dates, or details? Or are we supposed to work that out through dance as well?

LORIN. I'll go slow him down.

PIP. So he genuinely came up with that himself?

LORIN. He's been googling.

PIP *smiles.*

PIP. Please go find out the actual details though before he books us on a train for thirty minutes' time.

ACT ONE 67

LORIN. Yep, on it.

LORIN *exits.*

*

'D,

Forget all that. Living via your words is clearly working. Dad is trying. I can see through cracks in the walls to parts of him that you knew and loved.

Maybe Kew isn't the worst idea... I want your notes back though. I need to go in there equipped *with knowledge.*

Hold tight. I'm on my way.'

**

PIP *enters Lorin and Craig's room, heads to the wardrobe. They pull open the drawer, carefully, silently, looking for where the diary was placed. As they reach in, their face drops. Out of the drawer,* PIP *pulls out book after book after book. Years' worth, decades' worth of* DUNCAN*'s diaries. They stagger back, dropping the books to the floor, surrounded by them all, overwhelmed.*

Catching Up

Diaries and timelines are overlapping and catching up. PIP *is constantly picking up and tossing down diaries as they go – coming into themselves, confident, brash; annoying* CRAIG.

*

DUNCAN. *'20/07/1993*

Diary,

Lorin. Never take her for granted! NEVER. Angel she is.

She reminded me of my own words today:

Live out loud.

LIVE OUT LOUD.

I don't want to wilt and rot because someone else doesn't know how to look after the garden. I'm a seed on the wind! I've found new spots of sunshine, new pools of rain, all in the same garden I first took root in.

Five years later I'm just seeing it. Leaving Brum shouldn't have been the only way out. Weeds don't exist. They're just flowers someone has decided shouldn't be there.

~~Imagine your own brother thinking of you as a weed.~~

Although telling my clients weeds exist is what gets me half my work so let me not speak too soon. Had two prospective jobs today. Might ask Craig in to help with the heavy lifting. Good boy that he is.

Though Lorin would say:

TELL. DON'T ASK.

Move through this earth like it owes you something. All the straight boys do – why not us?'

**

PIP. Dad! Can I come with... I'm coming with you to the allotment.

*

DUNCAN. '*Officially move in with L and C tomorrow. I will miss you, little balcony.*

This is the last of it. However much my body creaks and aches and. I won't be uprooted again. I'm here and I am bright orange and I am out loud. Covered in bees.

D x'

**

CRAIG. Kale probably?

PIP. We should start tomatoes.

ACT ONE 69

CRAIG (*scoffing*). It's a bit early for toma–

PIP. Nah, earlier sowing gives them a longer growing period and a higher chance of fruit. We sow them under cover, keep them in that shed you have, plant out in a month?

PIP *hesitates, and then...*

Plant out in a month.

CRAIG *is left dumbfounded as* PIP *pulls on the jacket and strides past him.*

*

PIP. '*D,*

I still don't know what I was waiting for? I'm good at this!

I'm actually good at this shit without all the books and then with the books I'm fucking –'

DUNCAN. '*15/07/1993*

It's in the signals. It's not just about letting other gays know you're down for a kiss and a quickie, it's about letting other gays know we're here. *In numbers.*

Nobody wants to exist in isolation. Let the baby gays see you and know you and feel seen and feel known and feel empowered! Take Oscar Wilde – '

**

CRAIG. One seed per block, Pip.

PIP. And *then*! So they'd all wear green chrysanthemums in their lapels to *know*.

CRAIG. Interesting.

PIP. *Know.*

CRAIG. I know.

PIP. It's a whole second language, Dad. We're growing a second language.

CRAIG. Pass the cover, Pea.

*

DUNCAN. '*03/06/1993*

It's not about the clothes – it's about the layers.

That shirt? Put a scarf on it.

That scarf? Put a brooch on it.

That brooch? Own seventeen of them.

Coco Chanel said to take one thing off before you leave the house – well I hope that Nazi is spinning like a spirograph. I just put on three belts.'

**

We see PIP's *fashion changing here as they sift through pages and photos – from hiding in the background, to embracing colours and textures and styles.*

*

'*30/06/1993*

Diary,

Work is picking up – ~~I can barely keep up~~*, but my hours are spent mostly planning out my own dream, if I could ever afford the space.*

Daffodils, you can't have a green space that doesn't have daffodil bulbs hidden in every inch.

The same with crocus and hyacinth. Though I'm biased for the queers.

A garden without a traditional English rose is a cardinal sin – and I committed eight of those before my Ready Brek. If I'm having roses I'm having sunset explosions in messy, blousy, pillowy fireworks.

Clover, oh deep-red clover.

Weigela –

Sunflowers

ACT ONE   71

Rosemary all over.

ALL OVER!

D x'

**

1993, LORIN *comes out into the garden to see* DUNCAN *going at a plant in the garden that has been left to grow wild.*

LORIN. Not again. Come back inside.

DUNCAN. It's going to take over.

LORIN. It's the middle of the night.

DUNCAN. I need this space for the roses.

He swings around to shoo her away. He swings, stumbles, his body won't hold its ground the way it once did.

LORIN. Whoa –

DUNCAN (*shrugging* LORIN *off*). If I don't do this now…

LORIN. Leave it!

DUNCAN. You leave it.

LORIN. No *you* leave it!

DUNCAN. I can't! It needs tending.

LORIN. You have to see yourself in this moment.

DUNCAN. I do. I look good.

A beat. He does not look good.

LORIN. You look like you're at your limit.

DUNCAN. You haven't seen my fucking limit.

DUNCAN *returns to his work, holding back coughs, holding himself up. He stops, turns back to* LORIN, *who immediately goes to put her hands on his.*

*

PIP. '*D!*

I just thought this wasn't something I could do with truth in it.

But I am the truth in it.

I thought I had to carve out a space in this but this has to carve out a space in me.

Everything I reject –

Everything I am –

God it all flows queer, doesn't it?

How much work did they do to convince us queer was…

Well… queer.

Dahlia, honeysuckle, foxglove, jasmine. Evening air heady with me.

Look how I hold myself, look how the light arches its back to meet my face.

D, you've got me chin high, chest out.

Unapologetic and brand new.'

**

PIP *pulls out one last diary. They flick through the pages, a photo falls out. Small, slightly creased.* PIP *picks it up.* DUNCAN*'s beaming face looks up at them, stood against bright-white snow, adorned in the ski jacket.*

Oh my god.

*

DUNCAN. '*Mont Blanc, 1987 –*'

**

PIP. This is it. This is the holiday you all went on!

*

DUNCAN. '*Diary,*

Today was a dream. You should've seen me flying down those slopes. Barely had time for sleep – Jona took me out behind the chalet and –'

**

PIP *very quickly turns to a new page.*

*

DUNCAN. '*03/02/1987*

Diary,

Christ, what to do about Lori. Drama, drama, drama and if I'm being completely frank with you diary it's a bore.

I get running into your ex on holiday can't be easy, but to renounce your entire sexuality over it? I need to sit her down.'

**

PIP. What?

*

DUNCAN. '*Might go speak to this 'Elena' about it, though I don't want to overstep. Truthfully? I just want my holiday back! Drama is* fun *sometimes I admit but this is getting dreary.*'

**

PIP. Mum...

PIP *laughs nervously and shuts the book. Then thinks for a moment. Pulls it back open, reads furiously.*

Oh my god my mum is bi.

'*Facebook for Apple iOS, 2013*

Elena,

I've rewritten this I don't know how many times.

Maybe we could call?

I am so happy. I'd just like to know you are too.'

ACT TWO

*

'29/08/1993

Diary,

I think about what I am working to leave behind and it's all fucking flowers and foliage because flowers and foliage are soft.

Flowers and foliage are scented.

What if I have not crafted or curated or carved a version of myself that is worth remembering softly?

What if I had chosen a route of held tongues and stifled hearts? I would have been better in memory then, I bet.

I bet.

The only hands left to carry the reminiscence of me afterwards and <u>I feel volatile in them.</u>

<u>I</u> let <u>them</u> be soft. At my own expense.

Boundless possibility and all anyone cares about is who's a blossom and who's a brier.

Well.

Plants I hope my lungs look like: sea buckthorn, gorse, pyracantha, rose.

D x'

**

Patience vs Control

CRAIG *is proudly showing* DUNCAN *his attempt at an aquaponics set up – a hosepipe running from the pond (bucket containing maybe two fish.) with various nutrient gels inside.*

DUNCAN. And this helps how?

CRAIG. The water from the hydroponic aquaculture –

DUNCAN. Oh?

CRAIG. The fish pond.

DUNCAN. Oh.

CRAIG. Flows to the plant roots.

DUNCAN. Okay.

CRAIG. The level of nutrients is simply incomparable compared to growing straight from the ground.

DUNCAN. It's ugly, bab.

CRAIG. Gardening isn't all about frilly blooms.

DUNCAN. What did you call me?

CRAIG. It just needs more tweaking – see how it curves here? I'm sure there's a way to cut across –

DUNCAN. Craig.

CRAIG. It's taking too long for the water to flow –

DUNCAN. Craig – Craig. Craig my love, slow down.

CRAIG. It's just about efficiency.

DUNCAN. Okay –

CRAIG. You use fertiliser.

DUNCAN. I do.

CRAIG. So what's the difference?

DUNCAN. For gardening.

CRAIG. Which this is.

DUNCAN. Is it?

CRAIG. D.

DUNCAN. You are too preoccupied with function, you are missing out on emotion. Too focused on power, you are missing out on paradise!

CRAIG. And I get made fun of for my poetry.

DUNCAN. Feed yourself, nourish yourself, yes. But I tell you what – the colour of those crocus will linger in my mind ten months after the taste of those – what even is this? Chard? Long after that chard has gone.

CRAIG. And can the colour of those crocus keep you alive?

DUNCAN. Feels like it.

Beat.

CRAIG. Nothing wrong with function. I was reading about dark leafy greens – chard – they have magnesium.

DUNCAN. Good for them, bab.

CRAIG. Good for you. For your lungs.

Beat.

It's – lots of studies on it. On COPD and magnesium and I don't know.

DUNCAN. Thank you.

CRAIG. It's nothing, I was just overthinking probably.

DUNCAN. But I don't want it.

CRAIG. D.

DUNCAN. How about when I die you can scatter my ashes here and you'll grow the biggest chard this world's ever seen.

CRAIG. D!

DUNCAN. I wouldn't mind staying here. South-facing.

CRAIG. You're not – I'm not letting that – D, I can't do this, I need, just something, I need something, okay?! I need to fix something!

DUNCAN. Always the hero, right?

CRAIG. And you always have to be in control!

DUNCAN. I do not.

CRAIG. You do! Everything has to be your way or nothing!

DUNCAN. Sorry I have better taste than you.

CRAIG. You always have to be holding everything – running everything – in control!

DUNCAN. It's not control, it's agency!

Beat.

Please just stop trying to fucking save me like I'm some tiny porcelain baby

CRAIG. I – I'm not –

DUNCAN. You *have* a baby, Craig, go focus on that.

LORIN*'s head appears at the doorway.*

LORIN. Will you two shh!

CRAIG. We're fine.

LORIN. You sure?

DUNCAN. Oh here we go.

CRAIG. We're *fine*.

DUNCAN. Now comes Joan Jett to tell us that chard is a symbol of patriarchal resistance.

LORIN. Don't be a dick.

DUNCAN. I'll be what I want.

CRAIG. Some fucking appreciation would be nice, D. Maybe I got it wrong this time. But I'm trying. You're not exactly easy.

Beat.

I didn't mean that.

DUNCAN. You did.

LORIN. I think I'm going to go back inside.

DUNCAN. I think you two are happy I'm stuck here.

I think... I think you two don't work without me. And now I'm *stuck* in this house as a buffer between the two of you. It's my job! Full-time employment sitting in the friction of it all, the claustrophobia, the static in our arm hairs and dole out the words you two are holding back. And then! Oh god *then*! I am *berated* for it!! *Scolded!* I don't know. You two are just better when you have something to blame the strain of this house on. God knows I've got what – a month left at best, so good thing you have that fucking baby.

LORIN. Hey.

DUNCAN *coughs, his friends go to him but he holds his hands up to keep them back.*

DUNCAN. I didn't mean that.

CRAIG. Okay.

LORIN. I told you not to be a dick.

CRAIG. Lorin.

LORIN. I did.

DUNCAN. We barely have any friends left.

LORIN. I know.

DUNCAN. Why am I still here?

Bouquet of Violets

LORIN *is at the mirror in her and* CRAIG's *bedroom. She has just gotten dressed, and is applying moisturiser to her hands and face.* PIP *enters and hovers in the doorway.*

PIP. I like your top, Mum.

LORIN. I've had it for ages.

PIP. I know, I just like it. Very purple.

LORIN. What did you do?

PIP. Nothing!

LORIN. Hm.

PIP. A violet purple.

LORIN. I suppose.

PIP. Did you know violets were Sappho's flower? Like she wrote about them all the time.

LORIN. I did.

PIP. So like, if you are a woman, you could give another woman a bouquet of violets to let her know you were into her.

LORIN. That's nice.

PIP. Or wear violet…

LORIN. What?

PIP. Nothing.

LORIN. A bouquet of violets would be lovely, wouldn't it?

PIP. I could guess you'd like one.

LORIN. Pip?

PIP. Yes?

Silence.

LORIN. You're being weird.

PIP. That's transphobic.

LORIN. Stop saying that!

Silence.

PIP. One of my friends is trying to work out if she's bi or a lesbian.

LORIN. Is that why we're having all this Lesbos violet chat?

PIP. I guess.

LORIN. Well that's nice, that she can talk about it with you.

PIP. Yeah... I can imagine if you had no one to talk about it with it could be really confusing.

LORIN. If you ever want to talk about that – you know I'm here –

PIP. No, Mum, I'm not talking about me.

LORIN. Okay.

PIP. I'm definitely not talking about me.

LORIN. Okay!

PIP. Have you ever had to talk about it?

LORIN. With a friend? Not really.

PIP. For yourself.

LORIN. What's going on?

PIP. You never fancied giving anyone a bouquet of violets?

LORIN. Pip!

PIP. That's not an answer.

LORIN. Well. We all have phases and questions.

PIP. I think you had more than a phase...

LORIN. Excuse me?

Silence.

PIP. I understand exploring sexuality but bisexuality isn't a phase.

LORIN. When did I say it was?

PIP. You just said 'we all have phases'!

LORIN. And I'm not bisexual!

PIP scoffs. LORIN puts her moisturiser down, turns to face PIP.

I can't keep doing this with you. I'm trying to keep up. I'm trying my best to get things right but if I get stuff wrong just tell me outright –

PIP. This isn't about me!

LORIN. Well, what are you on about?

PIP. I know you're not straight, Mum.

Silence.

Why don't you talk about it?

LORIN. I don't know what you're talking –

PIP. I'm talking about Elena.

Silence.

LORIN. Have you been through my phone?

PIP. Your *phone*?

LORIN. What are you talking about?

PIP. What are *you* talking about?

Complete standstill, then:

LORIN. Everyone fancies girls sometimes – Everyone dates girls –

PIP. No, Mum. Not everyone fancies girls sometimes! /

DUNCAN. / No, Lori. *Everyone* fancies girls sometimes!

LORIN turns to face him. 1987. The living room of a ski lodge.

LORIN. Isn't there just – isn't there some fluidity to these things maybe –

DUNCAN. Christ, Lorin, when did you get so liberal?

LORIN *shoots him a look.*

Okay, okay. Sorry. What did she say?

LORIN. She asked me to leave with her.

DUNCAN. Typical lesbian, make eye contact once and then ask to flee the country together.

LORIN. D.

DUNCAN. Okay okay okay. So you're, what, leaving with her?

LORIN. No.

DUNCAN. But you have feelings for her still?

LORIN. I don't know.

DUNCAN. So you're breaking up with Cr–

LORIN. No!

DUNCAN. Bab, please catch me up then.

LORIN. I just – I want to understand myself and I don't know what this means like –

DUNCAN. You're with Craig.

LORIN. Elena just brought up things I thought were –

DUNCAN. Pick one.

LORIN. I don't know if that's what I'm asking...

DUNCAN. Your problem is solved if you just pick one, bab.

LORIN. I just think I'm more than – more than one – I don't know...

DUNCAN *scoffs. A look. He's waiting for it.*

What?

DUNCAN. Come on.

LORIN. What?

DUNCAN. You know what this is.

LORIN. What what is?

DUNCAN. This. This 'thing'. It's a 'thing'.

LORIN. It's a –

DUNCAN. You're bored.

LORIN. I'm *bored*?

DUNCAN. Yes. You're *cool*. You're a bass-guitar-waving record-shop hottie who's dropped pretty early on into a perfect, happy, comfy relationship – and it's left you *bored*, Lorin. It's human. Shake it off.

LORIN. This isn't new. Me and Elena dated long before anything serious with Craig.

DUNCAN. And now it's serious and you've found a way to keep things interesting again… Keep *yourself* interesting.

LORIN. We talked. For hours.

DUNCAN. Ooh. Gay.

DUNCAN *paces. He's working up to something. He stops. Faces her.*

Honesty?

LORIN. Honesty.

DUNCAN. This life isn't getting you very high up in the 'who's got it harder' shtick, god knows since you started hanging out with us. But this isn't something I can take off whenever I want and return to my cushty soft straight relationship and move in with my perfect man in suburbia and forget it ever happened. And you can use this 'sexy summer' to reminisce, and impress your friends back home, but I don't think it's your reality. This will be a blip to you. A fucking *blip*.

LORIN *hesitates.*

Sorry to be overly real with you, but I'm not going to sign off on this edgy-girl bisexual fling to induct you into the fag club for weekends.

LORIN. I –

He looks at her.

DUNCAN. You? You what? You want to get your perfectly manicured toes out and dip in and dip out of a violent reality I am buffeted by every single day?

LORIN. This is real.

DUNCAN. He's going to propose, you know.

LORIN *nods*. DUNCAN *laughs*.

LORIN. I just want to know what to do.

DUNCAN. And I'm not going to tell you that.

LORIN. Why not?

DUNCAN. Because I like my friends!

Beat.

I. Like. My. Friends. And unless you tell me you are truly *unhappy* with Craig, I will not tell you to do anything but go back to your room and forget about whatever fling Elena could or could not have been. God. 'Elena.' She's even got a fling-type name.

Beat. LORIN *is looking elsewhere.*

So. Are you?

LORIN. Am I what?

DUNCAN *raises an eyebrow*. LORIN *turns back. 2013.*

PIP. Are you?

LORIN. Me and your father are very happy, Pip.

PIP. That's not what you said to Duncan.

Silence. LORIN*'s eyes flutter behind her, for a moment, but he's gone.*

ACT TWO   85

LORIN. What?

PIP. I read it in his diaries.

LORIN. Your dad told me you'd found one.

PIP. No, the others. Dad has decades' worth of them stuffed in a drawer.

LORIN *isn't shocked, she's aware. Her lips pull tight, her hand rests on her own drawer where* DUNCAN*'s diary sits.*

I don't understand why you didn't tell me.

LORIN. I didn't *not* tell you –

PIP. So when I spent years crying myself to sleep every night because I thought I had no one around me who would get this? You didn't think maybe you should not *not* tell me then?

LORIN. You didn't ask me.

PIP. I was fourteen!

LORIN. And you wanted nothing to do with me! I'm only just getting you back, Pea –

PIP. You wanted me back, you got me back. Drop the bisexual memoir.

LORIN. I thought you'd know enough to have given me the grace to feel through this in my own time.

PIP. It's been twenty-five years!

LORIN. Since Elena?

PIP. I'm sorry, are their other names I should be noting down /

LORIN. / But it feels like D – it feels like yesterday – This was a moment between me and him, Pip.

PIP. You were the one who wanted me to know him. You said it yourself. You can't pick and choose which parts I get to know.

LORIN. He picked and chose which parts he wrote down! There was a way to have this conversation. This is not it.

PIP. Then how?!

LORIN. You're digging into things you have no context for!

PIP. And you handed me the shovel!

LORIN. Well then full stop – I'm not – I'm with your dad, Pip.

PIP. Oh my god you actually believe being bi ends if you –

LORIN *is silent.*

Mum, bisexuality has no end. It's a blessing and a curse.

LORIN. Well I'm not attracted to – in the same way as when I was young.

PIP. Don't lie.

LORIN. I'm not lying.

PIP. This is bullshit.

LORIN. Watch it.

> PIP *charges up past* LORIN, *to the wardrobe, and pulls the diaries out onto the floor around them. They thumb through the pages until they find what they are looking for.* LORIN *stands completely stunned, did she know just how many there were?*

PIP (*reading*). 'February second, 1987. Two red runs today – woo! Lori came to me, floods of tears, Elena our ski instructor is leaving and asked her to go with her. I didn't even register that was going on with them – clearly my gaydar is off kilter, I blame the jet lag –' blah blah blah yadda yadda yadda –

> CRAIG *enters, taking in the entire scene.* LORIN *close to tears,* DUNCAN's *diaries out all over the floor,* PIP *reciting from one of them.*

Oh! Here! This'll do it. '*Lori's convinced she's got to publicly declare her shiny gold bisexual card now. Says none have hit as hard as this. I've never seen her so distraught. She begged me not to tell him, I have no idea if she's leaving or not. I guess I'll update you in the a.m.*'

Does that sound like a phase?

Silence. PIP *stares at* LORIN. LORIN *stares right past them to* CRAIG. PIP *follows her eyes around to meet* CRAIG*'s.*

Dad.

CRAIG. What is going on.

PIP. I just needed to know him –

CRAIG. What is going on, Lorin?

LORIN. Craig.

CRAIG. Someone tell me what is going on.

PIP. I needed to know him, Dad. I didn't think I had anyone –

CRAIG. Give them to me.

PIP. No.

LORIN. Pip.

PIP. I have had a direct *link* to Black queer history, *my history*. It's important we talk about them, that was a whole generation just taken and my generation doesn't have –

CRAIG. How many times? Generations. Okay. Your generation, I know you lot love to talk. You love to go to therapy and share and tweet and talk. But your generation wasn't there. You weren't there, Pip. And I heard you about your queer histories, and I heard you about keeping those preserved. But you preserve the public, not the private. These are not yours. Give them to me.

PIP. So you can bury them in the back of a cupboard again? No.

CRAIG. You have absolutely no right to be touching them.

PIP. But you never made any effort to tell me about someone who could've been a role model in my life.

CRAIG. You're acting like a child, Pip.

PIP. Clearly I know him better than you did, or you'd get it.

CRAIG *is absolutely stunned. Silent.*

He's in here! And in here. And here. (*They tug at their jacket.*) The second I put this on I knew him. And as soon as I knew him, I knew who I would've been if he was still here. Why the fuck wouldn't you tell me? I think it's because reading these I know who *you* would've been too – how much better – Years and years of *life* in these pages and you're letting them sit in the dust and darkness –

CRAIG. Where I keep my friend's belongings is none of your business.

PIP. It is if you're shoving them back in there. Don't you see you're erasing him? You've even taken the one part of this house that could root towards him and filled it with concrete! No earth, no soil, no green. No branches, thorns, leaves, buds – nothing! Nothing but barren, blistering, wasteland! You know how many cuts and scrapes that concrete put on me? Because you wouldn't just go to therapy?

LORIN. You are just throwing words with volume and cruelty on something you cannot grasp. Christ, we've have been treading water for twenty years. You cannot know how that feels, Pea.

PIP. And how do you think it feels to grow up in a house on the brink of drowning and you have *no idea why.* No one will *tell you* why. If I don't speak then nothing gets said.

LORIN *and* CRAIG *hear it. We all hear it.*

Nothing.

You have the opportunity to let his life carry on and you're going to hide it away in a wardrobe. You're literally putting my queer role model back in a closet. You do see that, don't you?

CRAIG. He was never going to be a role model for you, you know why? Because he's dead, Pip. He's dead.

Beat.

Are we all happy now I've acknowledged my best friend is dead? Is that what this is about? My best friend is dead and my child thinks by not publishing his fucking memoirs I am erasing him! I can't erase him. That bit's already been done for me.

PIP. You're different. The two of you are different in here – (*Gesturing to the diaries.*) If you don't want to admit to erasing him, at least admit to erasing her. Hm? While we're talking about erasing queer role models from my life – Pouring cement all over us. How about knowing your wife was a fucking fairy just like me this whole time and nobody saying jackshit about it?!

LORIN. Enough! Look at the pair of you!

PIP is still, silent, CRAIG too. The two of them barely react. They stay that way for what seems agonisingly long. LORIN steps back, straightens her face, and leaves.

*

'01/09/93

Diary diary diary,

A fantastic dream last night. No plot to it, just swathes of rosemary growing in a scrub under my washing line, scenting my clothes. Sun beating down.

I still dream endlessly of my garden: my list seems too pedestrian. Too tame. Hit me when wafts of coconut from the gorse plants by the Kings finally made their way to my window.

Derek Jarman describes gorse as 'a blaze of golden flowers forced by the wind into an agony of weird shapes'. I find myself feeling like gorse these recent nights. Twisted branches wrung out like washing.

One other trait of gorse is its persistence in flower, even in the bitterest cold. So I'm trying to hold on to the blaze, not the agony. ~~It's getting difficult.~~

Let me become hardy.

I don't need full sun to blossom, I simply need earth to root.

I want to bend with the wind and meet its breath in configurations of resistance.

Cluster my blooms in spines so no one should damage them.

Let me be tall, wild, gnarled, scented.

^ ~~Craig would fucking love this~~

I only wish I had the time to grow into all these things.

D x'

**

Lorin and Craig in the Debris

LORIN *is sitting at the table. Shoes on.* CRAIG *appears in the doorway.*

LORIN. Pip's outside.

CRAIG. Are you okay?

LORIN. No.

A while.

They're not going to stop asking about him, Craig.

CRAIG. I just don't get it.

LORIN. You created a pressure-cooker.

CRAIG. The world is a pressure-cooker. I kept that out.

LORIN. There was a version of this where Pip grew up in a world drenched in him.

CRAIG. Oh, open the floodgates from day one? Offer no protection –

LORIN. It's not flooding, it's steeping. It's soaking. It's roots that have been allowed to drink and quench and fill themselves under a river that flows however it wants. You made a dam, and dams burst.

CRAIG. I wasn't the one that broke it open, then.

LORIN *thinks*.

LORIN. I thought I could do it brick by brick.

A while.

'If I don't speak then nothing gets said.'

CRAIG. I heard it.

LORIN. Twenty years ago or now?

CRAIG. Both. One a little louder, maybe. We do work without him.

LORIN. I know.

CRAIG. We just keep taking the path that's signposted as easier. It somehow doesn't feel easier.

LORIN. Then let's talk.

CRAIG. I said to Pip, 'I want to do right by you.' That hasn't gone away.

LORIN. I know.

CRAIG. And you, too. I want to do right by you.

LORIN. I know that, too.

CRAIG. Elena?

LORIN. Elena.

CRAIG. What Pip said. You could've told me.

LORIN *sits on this a while*.

LORIN. You didn't ask me.

CRAIG. Fair. Did Duncan?

LORIN. Duncan. From what Pip has taught me over the years? Was as lost as I was.

CRAIG. Did you talk about it? At all, after?

LORIN. Never... face to face. So maybe he wouldn't. Or maybe he would. Maybe he thought he had more time to tell me. Wishful thinking, probably.

CRAIG. Pip would've sorted him out.

LORIN. Maybe.

CRAIG. Remember when I said I didn't enjoy that film –

LORIN. *The Mummy*.

CRAIG. Yes – and they gave me a thirty-minute lecture on 'biphobia'.

LORIN. You're right, they would've torn him to pieces.

CRAIG. Never face to face?

LORIN. Never face to face.

CRAIG. You read them too.

LORIN. I'm not sorry.

CRAIG. I don't want – I don't need you to be.

LORIN. It was just one. Over and over. I need to see him, Craig. I need to feel him. I can't live in a house gutted of his existence. No pictures, no memories, no –

CRAIG. Can I speak now?

LORIN *shoots a look.*

Just – if we're – does the speaking take turns or –

LORIN. Go.

CRAIG. I keep being told this house has been scrubbed of him. And I – I don't – Do you not feel how this house is beaming with him every second Pip walks through that door? That child of ours is more of a reminder of him than any jacket, trinket or photo ten times over. I'm saying... I see him and feel him every single day.

LORIN. Don't you think I deserved to know that too, then?

CRAIG *nods.*

ACT TWO 93

CRAIG. Pip would've sorted him out, he would've sorted Pip out.

A moment. A thought.

They might've hated each other.

LORIN. A collision forming a black hole at the centre of our galaxy.

CRAIG. And they'd both find a way to /

LORIN. Make it *our* fault.

LORIN rests her head on CRAIG's shoulder. He wraps his arms around her.

CRAIG. All the scaffolding has really fallen down, hasn't it?

LORIN. It's time to actually feel this, Craig.

CRAIG. I know –

LORIN. It's been locked up too long.

CRAIG. I know!

LORIN. Then do it.

*

'I'd apologise to Lorin, if I could.

I could.

I should.

I don't want to leave without her knowing she's enough. She's always been enough.

D x'

*

'Facebook for Apple iOS, 2013

Elena,

I was given advice from someone who has since apologised for being wrong.

But I don't think that would've changed where I ended up, maybe the journey here would've been nicer. More apricot, less blue.

I said you came into my head the other day but in reality you have lived in my head every day. My child thinks I don't understand them and yet I'm questioning my whole self in the same way they are every second of it all.

I hope you're well. I am.

Lorin x'

**

Port Pages

LORIN *reappears with an ornate-looking dark bottle and two glasses, small crystal ones. One pristine, one slightly dustier? Faded? She is moving fast, with a clear end goal – as if she doesn't do this now, she never will.*

PIP. What is that?

LORIN. Port.

PIP. Port?

LORIN. Port.

PIP. Okay.

LORIN. And you're going to sit.

PIP. Isn't that what Tories drink?

LORIN. Just sit down.

> PIP *hesitates. A moment. They sit.*
>
> LORIN *pushes* PIP*'s chair to face out the window, then does the same to her own. They are heavy. It's an effort and a half.*

She squeaks open the bottle, pulls out the two cups, moving easily with the first, hesitating over the other, before placing it down in front of PIP.

LORIN *ushers to* PIP *to drink, a faint smile as* PIP *takes the first sip from their glass.*

PIP. What?

LORIN. Hm.

As they sip, she sips too, then some more, then some more, then some more until her glass is empty. She pours another. PIP *watches in utter disbelief, amusement, both?*

Duncan and I used to drink port together.

Another big sip.

It was our thing. We would heave our sofa to face the window, sit and drink port all night until there wasn't a secret left between us.

PIP *is silent.*

Not just our secrets, everybody's. We would sit and drink and laugh and watch the world rush by the tiny window of our flat and make sure that by the end of the bottle we knew any and all business that had come up since our last soirée.

PIP *sips their drink.*

(*Staring at* PIP *drinking.*) That was his glass.

PIP (*suddenly aware*). Oh –

LORIN. I told your dad it broke. In the move after –

PIP. Why?

LORIN. I don't know why.

I do know why.

PIP. Okay.

LORIN. I just. (*She takes one last big sip.*) Your dad got so much – his diaries, his clothes, his – hell, his Filofax – and

I know why, I understand why. He was his best friend.
But he *also* got the condolences, the 'I'm so sorries, the...
permission to grieve.

But he was my friend too. I lost him too. I needed one thing
that wouldn't be absorbed into the vacuum of locked boxes
and storage units your dad was creating. He was given so
much room to feel, so many tangible memories to hold and
squeeze and love and cherish and instead he locked them
away – and the one space he couldn't hide? Filled with
concrete. So. I told him the glasses broke. I just needed
something that was ours. *Just* ours.

PIP *awkwardly stares into their cup.* LORIN *refills them both.*

Duncan and I used to drink port together, and after he died
I sat and drank port by myself.

PIP. Mum –

LORIN. I would wait for your dad to go to work, or fall asleep
in front of whatever TV show, and I would push the sofas out
as quietly as I could, set our glasses out, fill them, and drink.
I told him all the secrets I had gathered, and I could hear
exactly what he'd say back.

LORIN *laughs quietly, like she can hear what he'd be saying to all this right now.*

Anyway, I couldn't bear to pour his down the sink afterwards
so I'd lift a corner of that fake grass and pour it into the
ground.

PIP. Poor worms.

LORIN. Lucky worms.

PIP. Maybe.

More silence; the two sit and sip. They are perfectly mirrored for the first time. It feels like a symbiosis.

LORIN. When you said that. That not everyone feels like that
for – you know.

ACT TWO 97

PIP. For other girls?

LORIN. Yes.

PIP. I'm sorry, I wasn't thinking, it just came out.

LORIN. Duncan said that to me. Those exact same words, *almost*. But with the biggest fucking grin on his face.

PIP. Really?

LORIN. Skiing – 1987, a bottle of port, and I told him about Elena and he said, 'No baby, *everyone* fancies girls sometimes.'

PIP *stares down into their glass.*

PIP. Is that all he said?

A beat.

LORIN. All I care to repeat.

LORIN *exhales. Puffs it all out.*

When I said you never asked. I did not mean *you*. I meant – I – The world never asked, Pip. Hand in hand with your dad and suddenly nobody asked any more. Do you get that?

There's a version of me I lost to the practicality of marriage. Don't take this the wrong way – I love your dad, I love this house. I just wish I hadn't left behind scraps of myself in order to find them.

So, when they all stopped asking, maybe I could've told them, but some days I just don't want to. Some days I feel like there's nothing to even tell. Some days I want to scream. Most days I want to scream, but not always about that. Nothing is final, Pip. Things move and change and shift and fade and – my – our sexualities don't exist in one or the other and that's final. For me it's day-to-day. It's not something you can put in a binary.

PIP. I can't believe you just pulled that out on me.

LORIN. It felt good.

PIP. I bet.

LORIN. Pea, there was a woman I was in love with. We were together for a year. I was young, but it was what it was. Love.

The two sip together again. The silence is warmer. Smiles turn into giggles, LORIN's giggles into tears.

PIP *is stunned, this is the first time they've seen their mum in this way. They get up and wrap their arms around their mum as she sobs.*

It's not – I lost my friend too. I lost. My friend. And it's so stupid now but at the time you have to know all I knew was, it was because he was – And I'm still here, so clearly I wasn't – I couldn't – I wouldn't be – I refused to be gone too.

LORIN *says this with tears filling her eyes, staring at* PIP *as if it was a promise she made to them, for them.*

The Last Supper Part II

1993. The living room. The aftermath of 'The Last Supper'. LORIN and DUNCAN sit back to back, feet up on boxes. LORIN is enjoying a carton of Ribena, DUNCAN has a glass of wine untouched by his side. CRAIG, adorned in rubber gloves, is picking up plates around them, his own glass on the side.

LORIN. Craig Craig Craig – the ladders are still out – could you please put that stuff up in bags?

CRAIG. What did your last servant die of?

LORIN. Not doing what they were told.

LORIN and DUNCAN high-five.

CRAIG. What's even in here?

LORIN. God knows. All the ski stuff, mostly.

CRAIG. Is my stuff in here?!

LORIN. Yes and let's hope it stays there.

CRAIG (*with a spin*). Style.

DUNCAN. Let me see!

> DUNCAN *holds the jacket up against himself.*
>
> Maybe don't put this too far away – might come back in fashion.
>
> CRAIG *scoffs.*
>
> I know what I'm talking about.

LORIN. Is anyone going to eat that last one?

> DUNCAN *puts it in his mouth – no hesitation.*
>
> You did not.

DUNCAN. Thanks, bab.

LORIN. You did not!

DUNCAN. What?

LORIN. Craig!

DUNCAN. What?!

CRAIG. What?

LORIN. D ate it.

CRAIG. The last one?

LORIN. Yes.

DUNCAN. Yes?

CRAIG. After Lori said she wanted it!

DUNCAN. No, she did not.

LORIN. Did too!

DUNCAN. You asked if anyone else wanted it!

CRAIG. You never actually take the last one when someone says 'do you want the last one'.

DUNCAN. That's ridiculous.

CRAIG. Thirty years ol–

DUNCAN. Hey.

CRAIG. Twenty-nine-and-one years old and you don't know basic manners?

DUNCAN. Don't say one thing if you mean another. You two are the mannerless ones. Buy your own After Eights next time.

LORIN. I bought those!

DUNCAN. You also bought this house and yet I'm clearly doing a much better job with it.

A moment.

Thank you, both, for tonight.

LORIN. Thank *you*.

DUNCAN. DJ Lori, impeccable as ever.

LORIN *mimics a record scratch.*

LORIN. Well then, Duncan, the floral centrepieces looked stunning.

DUNCAN. The garden I nicked them from isn't looking great though. And can we get one last round of applause for Mr Craig Shakespeare?

DUNCAN. One more for the road?

CRAIG. We've got a lot to clear.

DUNCAN. *We?*

LORIN. Oh read it again, Craig.

ACT TWO   101

DUNCAN. Come on, Langston. Encore time.

CRAIG *clears his throat, pulls out his little book.*

CRAIG. My nearest and dearest, all at this table,
Raise a glass, if you are able.
To a night to leave no word unsaid,
Nothing broken that isn't bread.
No long lost trinket still not found,
No shoulders without arms draped round.
My dearest friends, my darling wife,
Raise a glass to this life
Of simple joys, some lows, some peaks
All sealed up with lipstick on cheeks.
I won't go on longer, I see my wife is vex.

DUNCAN. And me!

CRAIG. Just allow me one more,
It's only the last supper until the next.

LORIN *raises her Ribena carton.*

LORIN. Till the next.

CRAIG *meets her with his glass of wine.*

CRAIG. Till the next.

DUNCAN *stays silent, but raises his mug slowly to meet theirs. A clink. The three of them smile, and drink.* DUNCAN *breaks the moment.*

DUNCAN. Now, out! The next hour doesn't concern you.

CRAIG. Can't I join one time?

DUNCAN (*and* LORIN?). NO.

CRAIG. I'm going, I'm going!

CRAIG *is pushed out the door.* DUNCAN *turns back to* LORIN.

DUNCAN. You do the chairs, I'll get the port.

DUNCAN *pulls the glasses out of the cupboard, and checks out the window to see* CRAIG *has left.*

LORIN *goes to start lifting and then catches herself and stops.*

LORIN. Um…

DUNCAN. Heave!

DUNCAN *is pulling chairs over.* LORIN *is pacing nervously.*

LORIN. Mike's getting the full Elton.

She gestures to her hairline.

DUNCAN. Heave!

LORIN. He fucked a doctor in Madrid.

DUNCAN. Typical.

LORIN. And also, Katya was the one that broke your sunglasses.

DUNCAN. She told me that was you!

LORIN. I'm pregnant.

Beat. A big beat.

DUNCAN. Whose is it?

LORIN. What the fuck do you mean, whose is it?!

DUNCAN *waits expectantly.* LORIN *chucks a cushion his way. D stops, takes her in, smiles.*

DUNCAN. A little you?

LORIN. A little me.

DUNCAN. A little Craig.

LORIN. A little Craig…

DUNCAN. Let's hope only a little.

LORIN. His cheekbones maybe.

DUNCAN. Wait, does he know?!

LORIN *shakes her head.*

Why the fuck are you telling me?!

LORIN. Secrets come here first.

A beat. DUNCAN *puts his hands to his cheeks. Big smiles.*

DUNCAN. Oh my christ, we haven't even opened the port! The port!

Turns back to LORIN, *eyes to her belly.*

Oh shit, the port.

Looking at her belly.

LORIN. To the teeniest tiniest secret of them all!

DUNCAN. You sure it's Craig's?

LORIN. Funny! Uncle Duncan.

DUNCAN. Duncle.

LORIN. No.

DUNCAN *laughs, goes quiet, staring into his glass.*

D?

DUNCAN. I'm just, I won't get t– (*He stops himself*). I'm just so *happy* for you, Lori.

The two hold each other's shoulders across the sofa. Forehead rests on forehead. CRAIG *rushes through the door.*

CRAIG. Sorry sorry I know I'm not allowed here I just need a –

His eyes catch their tear-stained faces.

Everything okay? Lori?

DUNCAN *nods at her.*

LORIN. Oh, go on.

DUNCAN (*zero hesitation*). We're having a baby!

CRAIG. We're –

DUNCAN. Well, you're.

CRAIG. We're having a baby?

LORIN. We're having a baby, Craig.

CRAIG. We're having a baby? We're having a baby!

CRAIG drops everything and jumps over the sofa onto the two of them, euphoria.

LORIN. Careful!

DUNCAN. Don't crush it!

CRAIG. We're having a baby!

DUNCAN. It's just a little pea!

CRAIG. A pea!

LORIN. It's bigger than a pea –

CRAIG. A petit pois!

DUNCAN. Pickney pois!

CRAIG. A baby.

LORIN. A baby.

DUNCAN. I just hope they have my eyes.

Iris for Craig

CRAIG *stands in the doorway, watching* LORIN *and* PIP. LORIN *sees him, stands up and leaves. A look to* CRAIG *that says 'your turn'.*

CRAIG. I'm sorry.

Silence.

Pea.

PIP. Yeah, I know. Me too.

CRAIG. It was scary, Pea. We didn't know what was happening, but we did. We did. It was just so much faster than you could imagine. So if I haven't opened up about it, it's because I'm still going through it.

PIP. Mum says you hide from it.

CRAIG. She's probably right.

PIP. Probably?

CRAIG *smiles*.

CRAIG. I – Your mum was pregnant, Duncan wasn't getting better, but they just kept sending us home? No matter how bad it got, they'd send us home. I saw what my father did when it was dark. He let it overflow, swirl around him, and he became cruel. I wasn't going to be that father for my child so things went into compartments before they could overflow. Everything has a time, everything has a place. If it's put away you can deal with it later rather than sooner.

He had plans. Not even big plans. Just plans.

I came in one morning – it was the last morning. He said to me, so calmly, such a throwaway, like we were in the kitchen or something, getting ready for a night out. He said 'Oh, Craig, can you do me a solid?'

'Call Wayne – and Jules, tell them I need to reschedule our lunch.'

And I did. And there was just silence on the other end of the line, until Wayne said 'Thank you for letting me know.' He knew. Thank you for letting me know. And I put that away, so that Duncan wouldn't see any more scared faces around him. So that your mum would have support. So that you – small and precious you, wouldn't grow up in a world ripped apart.

I'm sorry I kept him from you. It felt like protection.

PIP. For you or for me?

CRAIG *just nods*.

He *lived here*, Dad.

CRAIG. With us. And you. Feels like a different house. But no, he, uh –

CRAIG *pulls out his wallet, pulls out a folded, fluffy-edged piece of paper with a detailed landscape on it.*

PIP. Is that our garden?

CRAIG. Would have been. All of it, it was the one-year anniversary of… and I had it all planned out. I woke up early, I made Ready Brek – awful stuff, his favourite though. You loved it. I went down to the market and to the florist and to the next florist and the next one. I kept going until I found a bunch of purple iris bulbs. They were so unhappy looking, I wanted to get a bouquet of them but it was very much the wrong time of year. I came home, we had everyone round. Toasted to him, toasted to my pile of bulbs in the middle of the table, shared memories. It was the perfect day.

And then I went to sleep, and I woke up.

There's an awful thing about a year and a day, because in the 'and a day', that's when you are met with the crushing reality that the world is going to keep turning. You have spent the whole year thinking, if I can just get through this. Just get through to *one year*. And then you do it, and it's over and it's just a Thursday.

How could it be just a Thursday? I've completed the year. I've done it. I did the bit where he dies and it's done now, so why didn't he come back?

One month later, concrete.

PIP *puts their hand on* CRAIG*'s. A moment. They take* DUNCAN*'s design off him and investigate it.*

PIP. Will you read them now?

Silence. A thought's worth.

CRAIG. I don't think so.

PIP. Dad –

CRAIG. Doesn't mean they'll go back in the wardrobe. I just –
I think he told me everything he wanted to tell me. And
anything else I think he was probably saving for you.

PIP *smiles.*

Those queer histories you're always talking about.

PIP. So you do listen!

CRAIG. I'm trying.

Sledgehammer

CRAIG. Outside please. Both of you.

PIP *and* LORIN *follow him out into the garden. Resting against the wall is a sledgehammer.*

Put these on.

CRAIG *holds out two jackets: Lorin's ski jacket, and Duncan's. He pulls his own on, slowly, with care and certainty.* LORIN *pulls on hers, most of her focus at* PIP, *who is shrugging back into Duncan's jacket.*

And these.

CRAIG *holds out two pairs of safety goggles, and a pair of swimming goggles.*

We only have two pairs of safety ones – I don't think – I'll take them.

He stretches the swimming goggles over his head, they land in place with a twang slap of the rubber. The three stand across from each other, taking each other in, jackets, goggles and all. A brief giggle from LORIN *at* CRAIG's *swim goggles.*

CRAIG *walks to the wall, picks up the sledgehammer, and returns to the circle. Exhale. Inhale.*

Exhale.

Swing.

CRAIG *slams the sledgehammer down into the concrete below them.*

Exhale.

Inhale.

CRAIG *slams the sledgehammer once more into the concrete below them. It cracks, breaks. He holds out the hammer to* PIP.

PIP *takes the sledgehammer, wobbly on their feet but determined in their stance, they heave the hammer over their head –*

Exhale.

Inhale.

They crush it down into the ground. Once more, they heave the hammer up, and swing the hammer down, this time a deep guttural scream rips through them as they break through the concrete slabs below.

They hand the hammer to LORIN, *who swings it up over her head and down into the ground with little to no hesitation. She screams.* PIP *screams with her. Once more. Crunch. The two scream together as the concrete rips apart.*

The sledgehammer is handed back to CRAIG, *who swings and plummets the hammer into the ground over and over and over. With every swing, the three of them howl, scream, bawl, curse, let it all out as one collective mass. Concrete flies out around their feet – soft, loamy earth revealing itself with every crash.*

CRAIG's *screams turn to wails, as the edges leave his voice and he falls into sobs pouring out his throat. He drops the hammer, pulls off his goggles, and digs his hands through the earth they have exposed. Shovelling away hunks of fractured concrete.*

LORIN *runs to him, dropping to her knees as well to embrace him as they both cry.* PIP *watches, before crouching low behind the two of them, wrapping their arms around them both on the floor. The endless billows of Duncan's jacket enveloping them all as they cry.*

Breathing the Same Air

2013. In the garden. PIP *stands, their face in the sun, breathing it all in.* CRAIG *approaches, a diary open in his hand. He stands with* PIP *for a moment. Face in the sun too. He hands them the diary, open very specifically on one page.*

PIP *reads. And reads. And reads. Reads words written for them. Not just 'for them' but* for them. DUNCAN *enters. The two of them in the garden* together, *at last. As he reads this last diary,* LORIN *and* CRAIG *bring the garden to life around them, following Duncan's plans to the letter.*

DUNCAN. I do enjoy these moments that we get.

Just little scraps here and there

To be alone.

Just us two cotching.

Lush.

Oh, small baby, small baby.

What does this all look like to you?

Can you see the colours?

Or just shapes.

It's all just colours and shapes, isn't it.

Colours and shapes that make up

How something has changed

Emerged

Its histories

Its futures.

For example, I know that the person who lived here before you, killed the garden of the person who lived here before them.

See those scars that trace the back wall?

Ivy.

Nothing wrong with that. Everything is born from something dying.

I also know that in the future your daddy is going to have a nightmare trying to pull up all those dandelions.

In those ivy scars, you know what I see?

Tenacity.

Even after you rip me down, my footprints remain.

And those that know me will find me.

My scars will outlast me.

A witness, if you will.

Decades beyond my passing to the damage inflicted on me.

On us.

In the change that is left by me, I will scatter histories.

And I hope you find them.

If you want to find them.

This is the time of year you plant for the spring and summer to come. Something has settled in my stomach that tells me I will not get to see the fruits of the labour I put in now.

There is a saying: 'Blessed is he who plants trees under whose shade he will never sit.' Memorise that, yeah.

I know I can't plant for myself. But I see so many of us leaving, I worry future generations will not know I planted it all for them.

So, I wrote something. Don't tell your dad. I'll never live it down.

'Dig your fingers deep in the mud, little one.

Cake your nails in soil and clay

Know that the roots that tangle your knuckles, I left for you.

Know that the worms that jump out,

Writhing and churning,

I taught them to dance, for you.

Know that in every weed that bursts up,

Every vine that trails down,

It is me, knowing that no number of flowers will ever be enough.

So I brought some extras, there, for you.'

I was at peace

Content

with what I was leaving behind,

Until I met you, face to face.

And now I do not want to leave you behind, small baby.

I do not want that at all.

Oh, what a garden this is going to be!

The life it'll hold!

I am so jealous of all you will see.

All those shapes and colours.

One day they'll drive you crazy,

And they sometimes drive me crazy in honesty.

But know this.

Your mummy and daddy are two of the greatest friends –

Family.

I've been so lucky.

Up until now, I guess.

I'm also jealous you will get to see them live out their lives.

Make sure they live them well, yeah?

Yeah. Let me finish.

'Turn your chest to the sun, little one.

Go GREEN! Go GRUBBY!

(Try not to go too much like your dad.)

And most importantly, go well.'

You know, I do think you got my eyes.

You got something.

End.

A Nick Hern Book

Lavender, Hyacinth, Violet, Yew first published in Great Britain as a paperback original in 2025 by Nick Hern Books Limited, The Glasshouse, 49a Goldhawk Road, London W12 8QP, in association with the Bush Theatre, London

Lavender, Hyacinth, Violet, Yew copyright © 2025 Coral Wylie

Coral Wylie has asserted their right to be identified as the author of this work

Cover photograph of Omari Douglas and Coral Wylie by Courtney Phillip

Designed and typeset by Nick Hern Books, London
Printed in Great Britain by Mimeo Ltd, Huntingdon, Cambridgeshire PE29 6XX

A CIP catalogue record for this book is available from the British Library

ISBN 978 1 83904 367 3

CAUTION All rights whatsoever in this play are strictly reserved. Requests to reproduce the text in whole or in part should be addressed to the publisher.

Amateur Performing Rights Applications for performance, including readings and excerpts, by amateurs in the English language should be addressed to the Performing Rights Department, Nick Hern Books, The Glasshouse, 49a Goldhawk Road, London W12 8QP, *tel* +44 (0)20 8749 4953, *email* rights@nickhernbooks.co.uk, except as follows:

Australia: ORiGiN Theatrical, *tel* +61 (2) 8514 5201,
email enquiries@originmusic.com.au, *web* www.origintheatrical.com.au

New Zealand: Play Bureau, 20 Rua Street, Mangapapa, Gisborne 4010, *tel* +64 21 258 3998, *email* info@playbureau.com

United States of America and Canada: The Artists Partnership, see details below

Professional Performing Rights Applications for performance by professionals in any medium and in any language throughout the world should be addressed in the first instance to The Artists Partnership, 1 1-29 Smiths Court, London W1D 7DP, *tel* +44 (0)20 7439 1456, *email* email@theartistspartnership.co.uk

No performance of any kind may be given unless a licence has been obtained. Applications should be made before rehearsals begin. Publication of this play does not necessarily indicate its availability for performance.

www.nickhernbooks.co.uk/environmental-policy

Nick Hern Books' authorised representative in the EU is
Easy Access System Europe – Mustamäe tee 50, 10621 Tallinn, Estonia
email gpsr.requests@easproject.com

www.nickhernbooks.co.uk

@nickhernbooks